To Gemma
Love NAN xx
HAPPY BIRTHDAY

JUICING FOR HEALTH

JUICING FOR HEALTH

How to make **65 fresh and natural juices** for health, vitality and delicious drinking – with a fruit and vegetable guide and 400 photographs

Suzannah Olivier and Joanna Farrow

southwater

This edition is published by Southwater

Southwater is an imprint of Anness Publishing Ltd
108 Great Russell Street, London WC1B 3NA

www.southwaterbooks.com; info@anness.com

If you like the images in this book and would like to investigate using them for publishing, promotions or advertising, please visit our website www.practicalpictures.com for more information.

Publisher: Joanna Lorenz
Photographers: Gus Filgate and Craig Robertson,
with additional pictures by Janine Hosegood and Simon Smith
Stylist: Helen Trent
Designer: Nigel Partridge
Additional Recipes: Susannah Blake, Nicola Graimes and Jane Milton
Production Controller: Pirong Wang

A CIP catalogue record for this book is available from the British Library.

Previously published as part of a larger volume, *Juicing, Smoothies & Blended Drinks*

COOK'S NOTES

Bracketed terms are intended for American readers.

For all recipes, quantities are given in both metric and imperial measures and, where appropriate, measures are also given in standard cups and spoons. Follow one set, but not a mixture, because they are not interchangeable.

Standard spoon and cup measures are level. 1 tsp = 5ml, 1 tbsp = 15ml, 1 cup = 250ml/8fl oz
Australian standard tablespoons are 20ml. Australian readers should use 3 tsp in place of 1 tbsp for measuring small quantities.
American pints are 16fl oz/2 cups. American readers should use 20fl oz/2.5 cups in place of 1 pint when measuring liquids.

Electric oven temperatures in this book are for conventional ovens. When using a fan oven, the temperature will probably need to be reduced by about 10–20°C/20–40°F. Since ovens vary, you should check with your manufacturer's instruction book for guidance.

Medium (US large) eggs are used unless otherwise stated.

Always check the manufactuer's instructions before using a blender or food processor to crush ice.

PUBLISHER'S NOTE

Although the advice and information in this book are believed to be accurate and true at the time of going to press, neither the authors nor the publisher can accept any legal responsibility or liability for any errors or omissions that may have been made nor for any inaccuracies nor for any loss, harm or injury that comes about from following instructions or advice in this book.

CONTENTS

Introduction

Juices have become extremely popular in recent years. They fit neatly into hectic modern lives, enabling you to effortlessly incorporate healthy habits into your everyday routines. The main advantage of juices is that they are easy to make, quick, convenient and packed with rejuvenating, healing and revitalizing nutrients. On top of all this, they are also delicious, and a freshly made juice can feel like a real treat.

Above: Fresh drinks can be whizzed up in minutes with a juice extractor.

The Benefits of Juicing

While you can buy ready-made juices and juice combinations in the supermarket nothing quite beats the taste of a drink made at home. Freshly made juice drinks are also a more potent source of nutrients and certain combinations have specific health benefits. If you drink juices on a regular basis, you'll enjoy clearer skin, better energy levels and balanced overall health. It is also well known that the antioxidants found in fruits and vegetables work most effectively when they are consumed together, and juicing encourages precisely this.

Combinations of specific different juices can be used to emphasize particular flavours or effects in the same way that you would in cooking – sweet and sour, savoury and spicy, warming or cooling – but you can afford to be more adventurous than you might be with conventionally prepared foods. The juice of a fruit or vegetable often tastes much better than when the produce is cooked or even served raw. For instance, you may not particularly like celery as a vegetable, but juice it along with carrots and grapes or tomatoes and cucumber, and you get a completely different, more complex and utterly delicious taste sensation.

Even if you feel like going off the rails and indulging in extra ingredients, such as alcohol, the very fact that the juice is based on fresh fruits and vegetables means that you are still getting a wonderful boost of vitamins, antioxidants and minerals – healthy in anyone's book.

Preparing juices also has a psychological benefit. The very act of making a fresh juice drink can make you feel good – you will feel you are nurturing and pampering yourself.

Left: Let children get involved in juicing and watch them reap the benefits.

Juices are also a great way to make fresh fruit and vegetables more popular with children, even those who aren't keen on them in their natural state. Juices are great fun to make and to share: encourage your children to invent their own concoctions and join in the preparation, or share a juice instead of coffee with a friend.

The History of Juicing

As long ago as the 19th century, doctors and naturopaths were using fresh fruit and vegetable juices to improve the health of their patients. Many well-known pioneers were responsible for researching and creating the wealth of knowledge and evidence we now have about the therapeutic properties of juices. People such as Dr Kellogg, Father Kniepp, Dr Max Bircher-Bener and Dr Max Gerson all helped to popularize the notion of the "juice cure".

However, there is evidence to suggest that juicing is even older than this in the ancient practices of wine and scrumpy (hard cider) making. After extracting the fresh fruit juices, fermenting them into alcohol was simply a way of preserving the raw ingredients – and in those days drinking alcohol was safer than drinking water, which was often contaminated. The healing power of certain foods was even recognized by Hippocrates, who said, "Let food be your medicine." Indeed, since time immemorial, food, water and healing herbs have been the cornerstones of the healing arts.

The modern concept of combining juices to make delicious fruit drinks probably began with mixed drinks such as cocktails. For the more virtuous and health-conscious among us, however, non-alcoholic juices and blends have always sat comfortably alongside the bar choice.

We are going through a change in how we involve ourselves in our health. Reliance on prepared and fast foods has given way to a re-emergence of interest in healthy eating messages – the most familiar of these is that we need to eat at least five portions of fruit and vegetables every day. One convenient way of achieving this, in the context of our modern, fast-paced lives, is to embrace health drinks as easy-to-make snacks, quick breakfasts and fast, delicious energy and nutrient boosters. The introduction of advanced kitchen technology, such as blenders, food processors and electronic juicers, has made the preparation of fresh juices quick and easy.

In recent years, we have become more and more interested in natural ways of improving our health – echoing the thoughts and practices of the pioneering enthusiasts of earlier centuries. In addition to their more general health-boosting properties, juices are also used for specific cleansing and detoxing, for helping speed recovery from illness and as part of anti-ageing regimes. Some experts also maintain that juices can help prevent some cancers, although this has yet to be proven. There is no doubt however, that freshly made fruit and vegetable juices provide many of the essential vitamins and minerals that are vital for a healthy life.

It is not often that something so healthy also tastes so good and is a pleasure to incorporate into daily life. Perhaps this is why juices are standing the test of time.

Above: Raw ingredients that can be juiced provide all the vitamins and minerals you need to stay healthy.

Below: The process of making juices is as enjoyable as drinking them.

the art of juicing

Learn about juicing techniques and discover the best machine for the job and how to use it. Find out how to choose and buy the perfect fruits and vegetables and sample suggestions for tasty juice combinations. Learn how to decorate, garnish and serve juices as well as how to pack them with a vitamin and mineral boost.

Getting equipped

For successful juicing, you will need some basic equipment. The chances are that you will already own some useful items, such as a citrus press or food processor, but there are some more specialist items available that will make the job easier, quicker and much more fun.

Centrifugal Juicers

These come in a variety of designs. They are the least expensive type of electric juicer, yet are perfectly adequate for most juices. They have a pulp collector into which the fibre and pulp residue is ejected. Some come with a jug (pitcher) attachment that collects the juice; others require a separate jug to be placed under the spout. Centrifugal juicers work by finely grating vegetables and fruit, and spinning them at great speed, which separates the juice from the pulp. These juicers are good for extracting juice from hard vegetables and fruit, such as carrots and apples, and from leafy vegetables.

BUYING TIPS

When deciding what equipment to buy, think about what you want to make. Juicers are best for firm vegetables and fruit, such as carrots, apples and green leaves, but although they can be used for soft fruit, such as peaches and mangoes, they do not provide much juice. On the other hand, blenders are ideal for soft fruit and are a good alternative to juicers. Blenders and food processors allow you to retain all the fibre in your juice. Before buying, ask yourself the following questions.

- Is it easy to feed the fruit and vegetables into the machine?
- If you are going to make large quantities, does the machine allow you to do this? How much pulp residue is collected?
- Are there any awkward corners to get into when cleaning? Round containers are usually easier to clean.
- Is the machine easy to assemble and take apart?
- Are any parts easily breakable? Make sure that removable parts are easy to replace if necessary.
- Is a jug (pitcher) provided or will you need to get hold of a container to collect the juice?
- Does the machine have a see-through container or lid so you can see what is happening inside?
- Is the power of the motor suitable? Some models have two-speed motors; others just have one speed. Decide which you need.
- Do you need to be able to crush ice? If so, check that the machine is suitable for this purpose.

Masticating Juicers

These are more high-tech than centrifugal juicers, and also more expensive. Instead of shredding the produce they finely chop it and then force the pulp through a mesh to separate out the juice. Electric or manually operated, masticating juicers produce a greater volume of juice than centrifugal models and, because of the method of extraction, the juice contains more live enzymes. In addition to using masticating juicers to make juices you could also use them to make delicious nut butters, ice cream from frozen fruit ingredients and healthy baby foods. Some masticating juicers come with useful attachments for milling grains, otherwise you can buy the attachments separately.

Above: Centrifugal juicers are quick, easy to use and relatively cheap.

Food Processors

These multi-functional machines comprise a main bowl and a variety of attachments, some of which are supplied with the original purchase; others can be bought individually.
For making juices, the most important attachments are:

- A strong blade that blends medium-hard or soft fruit and vegetables.
- A centrifugal juicing attachment that turns your food processor into a juice extractor. This is not as efficient as a dedicated juicer, but is a good option if you juice only occasionally or have limited storage space.
- A citrus press attachment.
- Ice crushing attachments.

Blenders

These feature a plastic or glass jug (pitcher) placed on top of a motorized base, which powers blades inside the jug. Blenders are a good alternative to juicers. They work well with soft fruit, and berries and can be used to create delicious thick juices to which a liquid ingredient, such as water or a thinner juice, can be added. Some blenders can also be used to crush ice, but always check the instructions.

THE FIBRE ISSUE

Juices made in a blender are different from juices made in a juicer in one important way: the fibre of the fruit is is blended in, rather than being removed. Fibre is not only important for healthy digestion, but also for cardiovascular health, and for helping balance blood-sugar levels. When choosing equipment, bear in mind that fibre is valuable in the diet and, while juicing will not replace eating whole fruits and vegetables, blended drinks are nutritionally equivalent to eating the whole fruit. However, nutritional guidelines state that one glass of juice does count towards the recommended total daily intake of five portions of fruit and vegetables.

Below: Blenders turn soft fruits into delicious thick juices.

Above: Your food processor can be used to juice softer fruits like melon.

Citrus Juicers

There are three main types of citrus press available. You can buy electrically operated machines, which extract citrus juice into a container; hand-operated hydraulic presses, which squeeze the juice down into a container; and hand-operated squeezers, which catch the juice in the base and collect the pips (seeds) in a ridge. Citrus presses are perfect for all types of citrus fruit, but you may occasionally want to use a blender or food processor instead, so that you retain the fibre and pulp of the fruit.

Above: Hand-operated citrus squeezers strain out the pips and collect the juice.

Above: Hand-held blender wands are easy to use and very effective.

Electric Wand

These hand-held electric mixers are good for no-fuss, easy blending. Some models come with a variety of attachments for blending and whisking. You need to use an electric wand with a deep bowl, or a flask (which is sometimes supplied) to ensure the blended fruit doesn't overflow. If you are going to juice on a regular basis it is much more practical to buy a proper blender or juicer, but hand-held wands are perfectly adequate for blending a combination of soft fruits and liquid.

Below: Always use a good sharp knife to peel and chop fruit and vegetables.

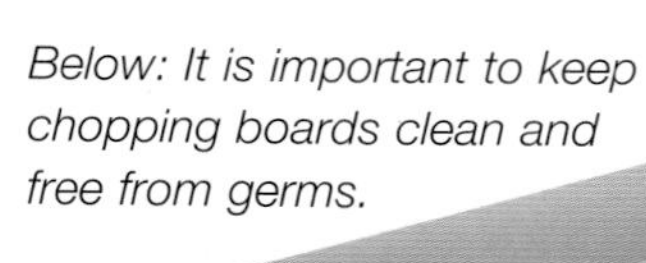

Other Useful Equipment

Chopping board Buy a big chopping board that will accommodate large quantities of fruits and vegetables. Plastic boards are easier to keep clean than wooden ones. To clean chopping boards, scrub with washing-up liquid (dishwashing detergent), then allow them to air dry – drying with a cloth often leads to recontamination. To avoid contamination, use a separate chopping board for fruit, vegetables and bread, and keep another to use only for meat.

Vegetable scrubbing brush Use a firm brush to remove dirt from your vegetables, particularly root vegetables, as an alternative to peeling.

Zester A zester is extremely useful for grating rind and adding intense citrus flavour to juices. The row of holes at the top of the zester shaves off thin shreds of rind, leaving the bitter white pith behind.

Canelle knife This tool has a tooth-like blade that pares off the rind in ribbons or julienne strips. Combined zester/canelle knives are also available.

Below: Citrus zesters and canelle knives are useful for preparing fruit.

Apple corer These make quick work of coring apples or pears before you blend them. Place over the core at the stem end and push down firmly right through the fruit, then twist slightly and the core will; come out easily. There is no need to core apples or pears if you are putting them through a juicer.

Sharp knife Make sure your knife is really sharp because this will make chopping much easier, and safer too.

Plastic spatula These are handy for scraping thick juices out of a blender or food processor, and the plastic will not scratch the equipment.

Below: It is important to keep chopping boards clean and free from germs.

Above: Use a large, elegant glass jug for serving your drinks.

Cherry stoner This simple tool takes the hard work out of pitting cherries and makes it much quicker. The bowl of the implement has a hole through which the cherry stone is ejected when the fruit is pressed.

Melon baller Insert this small round scoop into the melon flesh and twist to remove neat balls of fruit.

Above: A cherry stoner, an apple corer and a melon baller

Above: Sieves can be used to strain thick blends or to remove large seeds.

Measuring jugs Available in either glass or plastic and in many different sizes, measuring jugs (pitchers) must have the measurements clearly marked for ease of use. It's worth buying a large measuring jug.

Sieve This can be useful when you want to strain juices to remove seeds and pips for fussy children, or if you just want a thinner juice.

Vegetable peeler For preparing some root vegetables, such as potatoes and carrots, you will need a sturdy vegetable peeler. There are two main types available: straight blade or swivel blade. Experiment with each before choosing the one you feel most comfortable with, as this can make the job much easier.

Storage jug or vacuum flask
Choose a storage jug (pitcher) with a close-fitting lid or place clear film (plastic wrap) over the opening before securing the lid. Covering the juice securely limits its exposure to oxygen and prevents it from oxidizing. Even better, use a vacuum flask.

Serving jugs and glasses Buy different shapes and colours and have some fun with these, contrasting them with the colour of the juice you are serving. It is also useful to have a large glass jug from which to serve juices and drinks. Both the jug and the serving glasses will look more attractive (and be more hygienic) if they are really clean and sparkling. Wash them in hot water, rinse, and then dry with a clean, lint-free glasscloth.

Above: For exact amounts, use a set of measuring jugs and spoons.

Above: There are many different types of vegetable peeler.

Straws and swizzle-sticks
These decorative items are used to add the finishing touches to a drink and can add an element of fun to presentation. They are particularly effective for party drinks.

Juicing techniques

Once you have purchased the necessary equipment for juicing you will want to get started as soon as possible. For maximum freshness and flavour, prepare the fruit and vegetables just before you are ready to juice them. There are slightly different requirements for preparing produce for each type of machine. Always read the equipment manufacturer's instructions first.

Centrifugal and Masticating Juicers

Although centrifugal and masticating juicers function in different ways, the preparation of fruits and vegetables, and the basic principles for using the machines, are much the same.

1 It is generally better to choose firm produce for centrifugal and masticating juicers as soft fruits will not give as successful results. For instance, firm, underripe pears work well, but soft, ripe pears are better prepared in a food processor or blender.

2 Scrub any produce you are not going to peel with a hard brush under cold running water to get rid of any dirt. If there is a waxy residue, then use a small amount of soap or washing-up liquid (dishwashing detergent) to help remove this, then rinse the produce thoroughly under cold running water.

3 Prepare the produce. Most fruit and vegetables do not need to be cored or peeled – although you might prefer to core fruit – as peel, pips (seeds) and core will simply be turned into pulp and be removed by the machine.

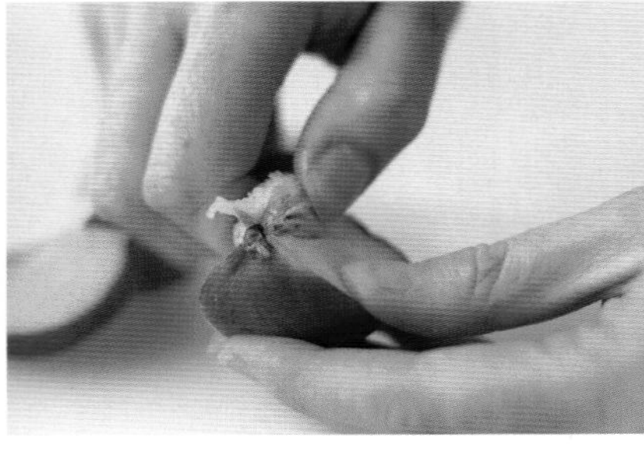

4 Large stones (pits) of fruit such as peaches and plums need to be removed. Cut round the middle of the fruit, using a small, sharp knife, then cut around again and seperate into quarters, then pull out the stone. Mangoes have a large, flat stone. Peel the fruit, then cut the flesh away from either side of the stone, then remove as much flesh as possible from the stone.

5 All leafy vegetables, such as cabbages and lettuces, can be put through a juicer. Include the outer leaves, which are nutritionally superior, although these must be washed thoroughly first.

6 Citrus fruit can be put through a juicer. Ensure that you remove all the peel, but there is no need to remove the pips (seeds) or pith.

7 When pushing the produce through the feeder tube of the machine, it is very important that you use the plunger provided. Remember to position a jug (pitcher) or glass under the nozzle of the machine to catch the juice, otherwise it will spray all over the work surface.

8 Put the ingredients through the machine in manageable quantities. Cut pears and apples into quarters, for example, and alternate them if possible to ensure that the juices mix well. If you push too many pieces of fruit or vegetable through in one go, or push through pieces that are too large, the machine will clog up.

9 Push through a hard ingredient, such as a carrot, after softer ingredients, such as cabbage. This will keep the juice flowing freely and will prevent blockages.

Cleaning Juicers, Blenders and Food Processors

The one and only dreary thing about making delicious fresh juices is that the equipment needs to be cleaned soon afterwards. However, there are some simple, no-fuss ways of making this chore much easier.

Cleaning a juicer, blender or food processor thoroughly is important if you want to avoid unwanted and unhealthy bacteria, and the best time to do this is straight after you have made the juice and poured it into glasses or a jug (pitcher). If you clean the parts of a juicer, blender or food processor immediately (or better still put to soak in water), the pulp and residue should just rinse off easily.

1 To clean a centrifugal or masticating juicer, blender or food processor, fill a sink with cold water and carefully take the equipment apart, following the manufacturer's instructions.

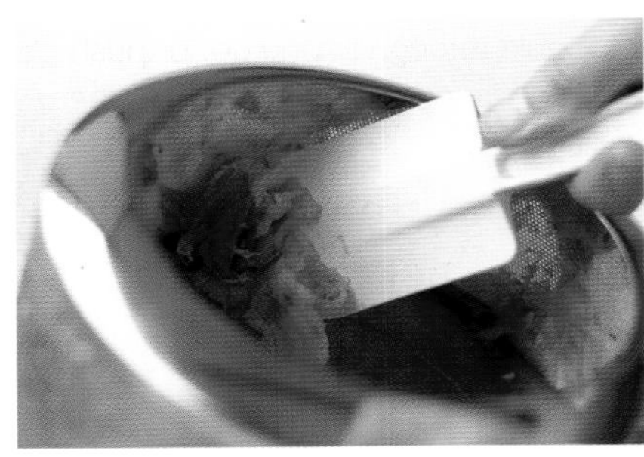

2 Using a plastic spatula or spoon, scoop off any large pieces of residue (such as the fruit and vegetable pulp that collects inside the spout of the juicer or around the blades) and discard it. Better still, if you have a compost heap in the garden, add the fruit or vegetable residue to it.

3 Plunge the non-electrical, removable machine parts of the juicer, blender or food processor into the sink full of cold water and leave them to soak until you are ready to clean them – this will probably be after you've sat back and enjoyed your freshly made juice. Soaking the machine parts will help to loosen any remaining fruit and vegetable pulp and will make cleaning them much easier.

4 After soaking, either carefully handwash the non-electrical, removable machine parts or put them into a dishwasher on a normal setting.

5 Scrub any attachments that you have used with a firm brush to loosen any residue that remains. Take care when handling grating attachments as they are extremely sharp.

6 The removable components of your juicer, blender or food processor may occasionally get stained, especially if you regularly make juices with vibrantly coloured ingredients such as blackberries or beetroot. Soak these stained components every now and then in plenty of cold water with a little bleach added. Be sure to rinse the parts thoroughly afterwards, then leave them until they are completely dry before putting the machine back together.

TROUBLESHOOTING

If you experience any problems using your juicer, or if the resulting drink is not quite what you imagined, the following may help.

The machine gets clogged up

Push a hard fruit or vegetable, such as a carrot or apple, through the machine to keep the juice flowing.

The taste of one ingredient is overwhelming the juice

Increase the quantity of another ingredient, use a base juice to dilute the flavours or add a splash of lemon or lime juice to help rescue the juice.

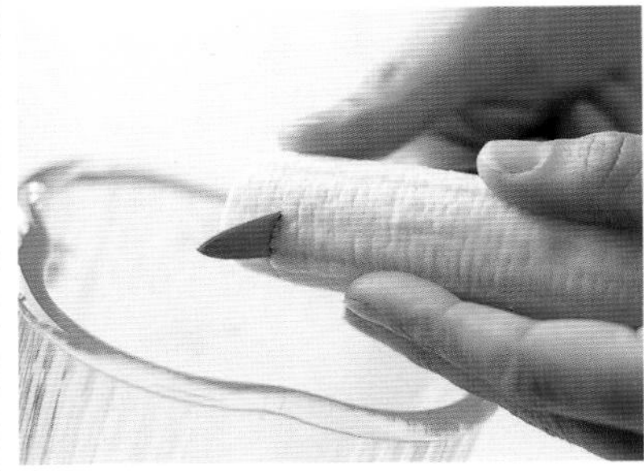

The blend is too thin

Add an ingredient to thicken the juice drink, such as banana or avocado.

TROUBLESHOOTING

If you experience any problems using a blender or food processor, or if the resulting drink is not quite what you imagined, the following may help.

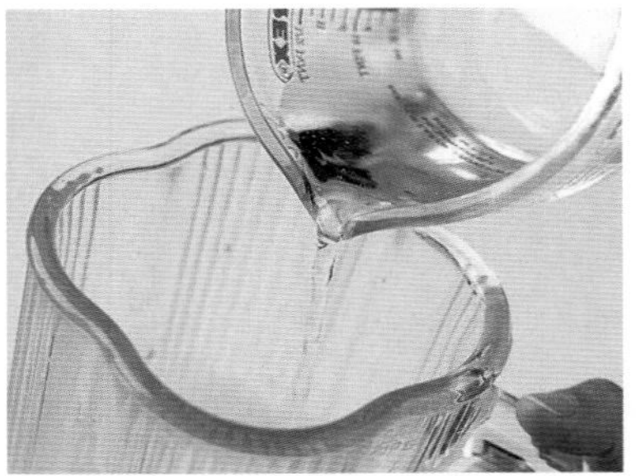

The blend is too thick

Thin it using water or the juice of a watery fruit. For a pure taste, use fruit juice to dilute a fruit purée made in a blender.

The blend is too pulpy

Strain the mixture through a sieve, pressing the pulp down with the back of a spoon.

The ingredients get stuck to the side of the bowl

Scrape down the mixture with a plastic spatula to ensure that all ingredients are mixed thoroughly.

Blenders and Food Processors

These machines work in fairly similar ways, and the preparation of fruit is the same for both types of equipment. The main difference is the point at which you add liquid. Blenders and food processors are best used for soft fruits.

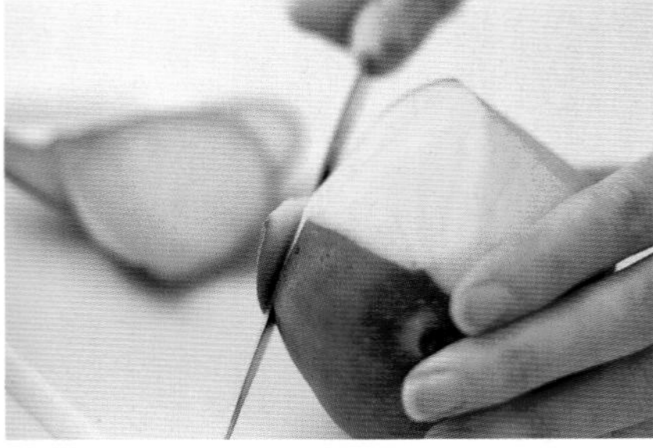

1 Fruits with inedible skins, such as bananas, mangoes and papayas, should be peeled.

2 Fruits with edible skins, such as peaches or plums, do not need to be peeled but should be washed thoroughly. If you prefer a juice with a finer, smoother texture, peel the fruits before blending.

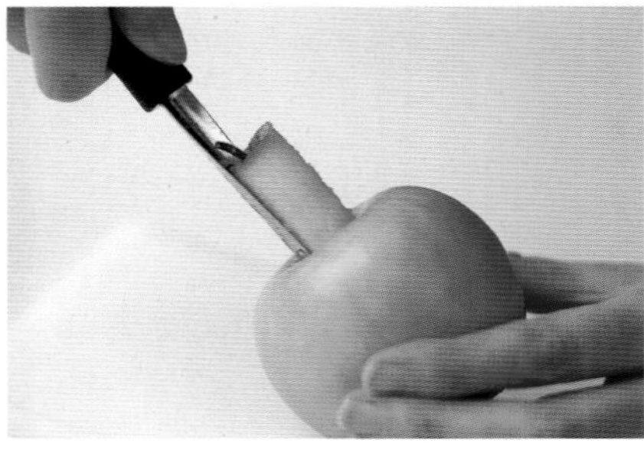

3 Fruits with large stones (pits), cores or pips (seeds), such as mangoes, plums, cherries and apples, should be stoned (pitted), cored or seeded.

4 Fruits with tiny seeds, such as raspberries, strawberries or kiwis, can be used whole, when the seeds add texture and a pretty speckled effect. However, if you prefer a smooth drink, the blended pulp can be pushed through a fine sieve, using a plastic spatula, to remove the seeds.

5 When using berries and currants, remove the stalks and leaves and wash the fruit thoroughly. An easy way to detach, or string, redcurrants, blackcurrants or whitecurrants from their stalks is to hold the bunch firmly at the top, then slowly draw the tines of a fork through the fruit so that the currants fall away.

6 To juice fruit in a food processor, place it in the bowl of the machine and process until it is a thick pulp. Then add a liquid ingredient such as water or fruit juice and process the juice again.

7 To juice fruit in a blender, it is important to add the liquid ingredients and the soft fruit at the same time, then process all together, otherwise the blades will not be able to blend the fruits effectively.

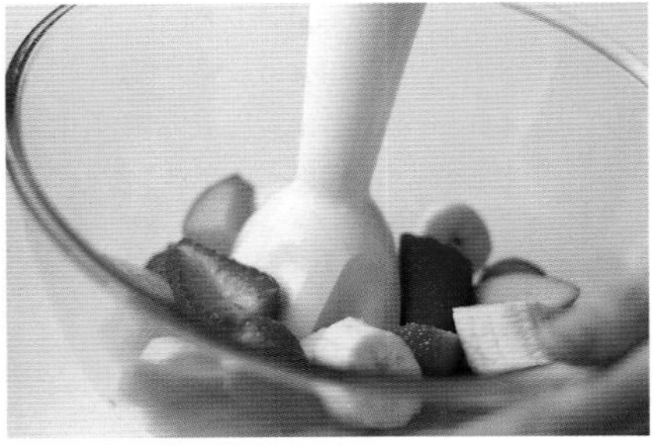

8 If using a hand-held electric wand, remember that this piece of equipment is not as powerful as other juicers or blenders. Use only very soft fruits, such as bananas, peaches and berries, as it cannot cope with anything firmer.

Citrus Juicers

1 First, cut the citrus fruit in half using a sharp knife.

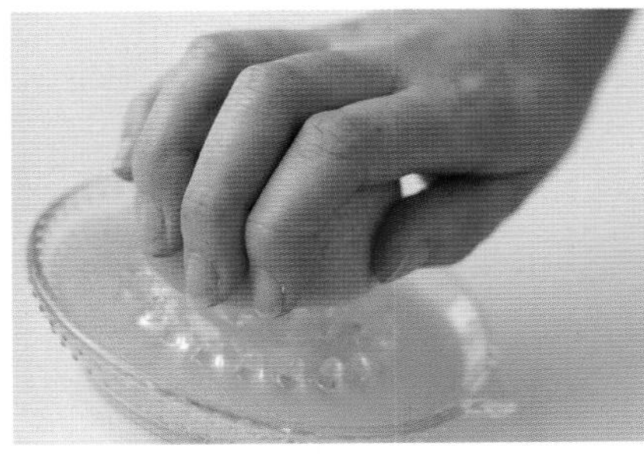

2 To use a traditional juicer, press the cut half over the cone of the juicer and, using an even pressure all round, twist the fruit to squeeze out as much juice as possible. The rim of the squeezer will catch any pips (seeds) and the surrounding bowl will catch the juice.

3 To use a juicer with a citrus attachment or an electrically operated citrus juicer, firmly press the halved fruit over the spinning cone of the juicer. The motor will turn the cone under the fruit, and this will extract more juice than a simple manual juicer would usually produce.

4 To use a manual hydraulic press, place a container under the juice nozzle to collect the juice (unless one is supplied as part of the juicer) and place the halved citrus fruit in the press. Pull the lever forwards to apply pressure and squeeze out the juice.

5 To use a centrifugal or masticating juicer, remove the citrus peel with a sharp knife (there is no need to worry about removing the pips or the white pith that remains). Cut the fruit into similar-sized chunks or break into segments, then press the fruit through the juicer funnel.

QUICK START TIPS

If you are impatient to get going, you can achieve some delicious instant results with one of these simple basic juices.

Pear and Cucumber Juice

½ small cucumber
1 large pear
ice cubes

Roughly chop the pear into chunks. Peel and chop the cucumber and juice both together. Pour into a glass with ice cubes and serve.

Carrot and Apple Juice

2 large carrots
1 apple

Wash the carrots and apple, cut into chunks and push through a juicer. Spoon off any foam, if you prefer and serve

Lemon and Orange Refresher

1 orange
½ lemon
sparkling water
5ml/1 tsp sugar (optional)
ice cubes and/or fresh mint leaves

Juice the fruit in a juicer. Add the sparkling water and sugar, if using. Pour into a glass, add ice cubes and/or mint leaves, then serve.

Tomato and Pepper Boost

½ red (bell) pepper
150g/5oz tomatoes
juice of ½ lime
ice cubes

Soak the tomatoes in boiling water, then peel off the skin and chop into chunks. Halve the red pepper, remove the seeds and chop into similar-sized chunks. Add the pepper and tomatoes to a blender or food processor and blend well. Add a squeeze of lime juice and some ice cubes, then serve.

Serving, decorating and storing juices

The ideal way to enjoy juices is to drink them immediately. This way you benefit from the full flavour and nutritional benefits, because time and exposure to oxygen take their toll on the nutrient content of most prepared fruits and vegetables. For instance, when you make carrot juice, it is a bright orange colour, but if you leave it for an hour it will turn brown as it oxidizes. Likewise, the flesh of apples or avocados turns brown as it oxidizes and loses nutritional value.

Serving and Decorating Juices and Drinks

There are many attractive and quirky ways to serve fresh drinks. With a little forethought and imagination, you can present friends and family with gorgeous-looking concoctions – whatever the occasion.

Adding ice Ice is a wonderful addition for, cooling, decorating and even flavouring drinks. Simple cubes are good for cooling drinks, but these can also be decorated or flavoured in a number of different ways. Crushed ice is a good way to cool drinks, with a more immediate effect than ice cubes.

Juicy ice cubes Make cubes from orange, cranberry or diluted lime juice in an ice-cube tray. These will create a rainbow effect in your drinks and will also alter the taste as they melt.

Right: Suspend sprigs of currants over your drinks for a stunning effect.

Fruit ice cubes Place raspberries or other small fruits in an ice-cube tray and add water.

Fruit purée drizzle For a striped effect, pour fruit purée down the inside of glasses before adding the drink.

Flower and petal ice cubes Choose flowers that are edible and will be attractive even when the ice has melted – rose petals, pinks or borage.

Sugar-rimmed glasses Moisten the rim of a glass with water, dip into grated lemon or lime rind and then into icing (confectioners') sugar.

Edible swizzle sticks These can be fun and celery sticks are a natural choice for savoury drinks. Finely slice one end of the stick, then soak in iced water for about 15 minutes – a fanned-out fringe will develop.

Fruit skewers Place fruit segments or currants on a skewer and use as a swizzle stick. Bruised lemon grass stalks, lavender or rosemary stems, or cinnamon sticks can also be used.

Glass decorations Place fruit slices on the rim of a glass or skewer small pieces of fruit on to cocktail sticks (toothpicks) and balance these across the tops of glasses. Experiment with herb leaves and pared citrus rind.

Ice lollies Fruit juices make healthy ice lollies (popsicles) for children. All you need is an inexpensive mould, available from kitchenware shops. This is a fun way to serve juice at parties.

Above: To make children's parties fun, try serving fresh juices frozen into lollies.

Storage of Juices and Drinks

While it is definitely best to serve juices when they are just freshly made, you may want to store them for one reason or another. Perhaps you have made too much to drink in one go, maybe you have a glut of berries or some other produce that you need to use up before it over-ripens, or you might simply want to take a home-made juice into work for a healthy mid-morning snack.

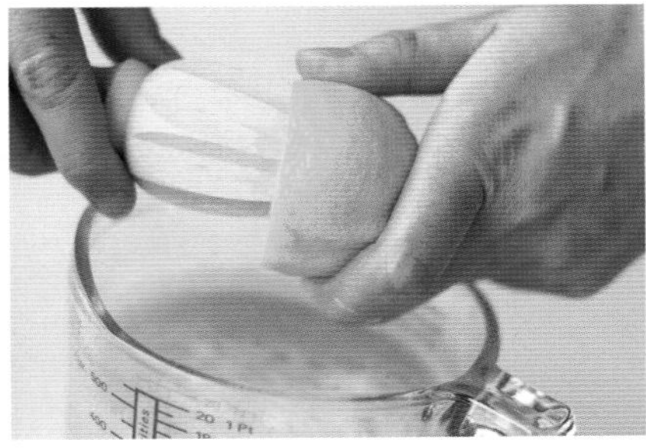

One way to minimize the oxidization of juices is to add some vitamin C. Either squeeze in a little fresh lemon or orange juice or add 2.5ml/½ tsp of powdered vitamin C, which is available from health food stores. Juices can then be stored in the refrigerator for a few hours and won't discolour – make sure you chill them as soon as possible after making.

To store a juice pour it into a jar or jug (pitcher), filling it right to the brim. Seal with clear film (plastic wrap) or, alternatively, use a screw-top jug or vacuum flask.

Most juices can be frozen for use at a later date and this will preserve almost all of their full nutritional value. Try freezing different flavoured juices in ice-cube trays – the ice cubes can then simply be removed and added to drinks. Otherwise, try to freeze the juice in fairly small amounts (glassfuls). Any juice or fresh drink can be frozen successfully, but it is a good idea to make single ingredient base juices to freeze, because you can then add different flavourings when the juice is thawed. Make sure you label and date the containers clearly.

Buying produce

If you are really enthusiastic about making juices and fresh drinks you may want to bulk buy some of the basic ingredients. Carrots, apples, bananas, pineapples and oranges are often used as base juices to which other ingredients are added. Additional ingredients, such as summer berries, are best used when really fresh and so should be juiced on the day of purchase.

Above: Buy produce that is ripe if you can, but if it is needs further ripening, simply leave it on a sunny windowsill.

Freshness

The produce you use when making juices, should be as fresh as possible to ensure that you will get the maximum nutrients from your drinks. It is not necessary to buy produce that looks perfect, – if it is damaged you can easily remove the affected parts. Aim to buy fruit and vegetables that are in season if you can. If you can buy seasonally and locally, your fresh produce will be bursting with health-boosting vitamins and minerals.

Locally grown food is more nutritious than food that has been imported from abroad. Fruit and vegetables for export are often picked before they are fully ripe and kept chilled to avoid spoilage. This means they fail to develop the complex flavours and nutritional compounds available in produce that has been left to ripen naturally.

Ripeness

The riper the fruit, the more sugar it will contain and the sweeter it will be. It also means that the fruit contains more nutrients, especially if the produce has been ripened on the tree or plant. Fruits that are picked green and ripened in transit contain fewer nutrients.

Storage

All fruit and vegetables benefit from being stored in cool, dry conditions. However, if fruit is slightly underripe and too firm to be juiced, find a sunny windowsill on which to ripen it for a couple of days. Ripe fruit, particularly bananas, will give off a gas that speeds up the ripening of any fruit stored alongside it. Avoid wrapping produce in plastic bags as it cannot breathe. Also it's best not to store fruit alongside strongly flavoured vegetables, such as onions, as the fruit can take on the flavour.

Organic Produce

Food that is grown organically is slightly more expensive than regular produce, but there are some clear advantages in choosing it.

Organic produce is good for you. Fresh organic fruit and vegetables contain more vitamins, minerals, and enzymes than intensively farmed produce. The levels of chemicals that you are exposed to via pesticides, fungicides and herbicides will be significantly reduced if you choose organic produce. Advocates of organic fruit and vegetables also claim that they taste better because there is less water

Left: Organic fruits tend to contain less water so the taste is more intense, and they are not sprayed with pesticides.

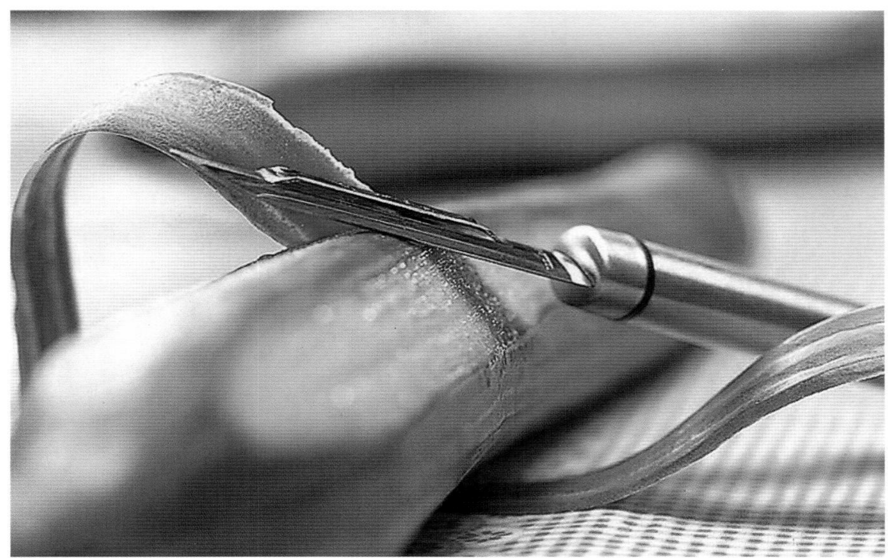

Above: It may be worth peeling the skin of non-organic produce, as this will remove any possible chemical residue.

bulking out the produce. It is certainly true that if you taste an organic carrot and then compare it to the taste of a non-organic carrot, the former will usually have a more solid texture and a stronger, more intense carroty taste. This inevitably means that your drinks will have more flavour, as there will be less water diluting the juice.

Even if you don't want to buy entirely organic produce, you may want to consider buying bulky base items, such as carrots and apples, from organic ranges.

Convenient Options

For convenience, and because you can't always find fresh produce out of season, it is worthwhile keeping some dried, frozen, canned and bottled fruits or vegetables to hand in your store cupboard (pantry). Use these as substitutes whenever you run out of a fresh ingredient or if you find that an ingredient is unavailable or out of season. Choose fruits that are preserved in unsweetened fruit juice in preference to syrup, as this is a more healthy option. Dried apricots, dates and figs can also be useful

Frozen fruit such as strawberries, raspberries, blueberries and bags of frozen mixed summer fruits can work very well in fresh juice drinks. If blended straight from the freezer, they turn a juice into a deliciously chilled slush and you will not need to add any additional ice.

IRRADIATION

Most herbs and spices are irradiated (treated with radiation to delay spoiling) but this is forbidden with organic produce. If you wish to avoid irradiated herbs and spices you need to buy organic produce.

GM CROPS

Genetically modified foods are a recent innovation. If you have concerns about this type of produce, buy organic fruit and vegetables. Also, look in your local health food shop and choose only products that state they contain non-genetically modified ingredients.

Below: To avoid genetically modified produce, buy organic – it is worth spending a little bit more.

Citrus fruit

To juice citrus fruits you will need to use a citrus juicer, and the juice can then be added to other blends if desired. Oranges are available all year round and store well in cool, dry conditions. All citrus fruits are rich in vitamin C, and one large orange provides your recommended daily allowance (RDA). Oranges, tangerines, mandarins and other citrus fruits are also excellent sources of folic acid. As an alternative to using a citrus juicer, you could push the peeled fruit through a juicer to benefit from the fibre and pith. The pith is rich in two bioflavonoids, rutin and hesperidin, which aid the absorption of vitamin C and strengthen blood vessels. The rind is rich in limonene, which is very good for liver health. However, some people find that certain citrus fruits are too acidic for their digestive system.

Preparing and Juicing Citrus Fruits

To juice citrus fruits, you will need a citrus juicer (hand-held, electric or hydraulic), a chopping board and a sharp knife. If you are going to use the rind, you will also need a scrubbing brush, soap or washing-up liquid (dishwashing detergent), and a grater.

Juicing The simplest way to juice citrus fruits is to cut them in half and squeeze out the juice using a hand-held juicer or a reamer. A hydraulic citrus press or citrus attachment on an electric juicer is more efficient, however, and will produce more juice. Press the cut fruit against the cone of the juicer. Peeled fruits can also be juiced in a juicer or blended using a food processor or blender.

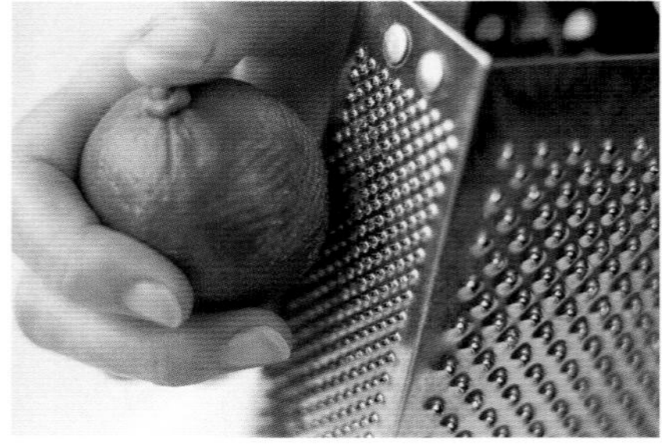

Grating rind If you wish to use rind in a juice, choose a non-waxed organic fruit to avoid chemical residue or scrub the skin with a firm brush using a little soap, then rinse. Grate on the fine mesh of your grater or use a zester.

Oranges

These are generally sweet, although some have a sharper flavour than others. Always choose eating oranges for juicing; Seville (Temple) oranges are too bitter. Blood oranges are sweeter than regular oranges and produce a lovely ruby-red juice.

Oranges are often used to make a base juice to which other juices can be added and combined. To tone down the sweetness of orange juice, add grapefruit juice or dilute with water. Orange juice goes well with most other juices, particularly carrot and lemon.

Therapeutic uses Orange juice is often used as a cold and flu remedy. It is rich in folic acid, which is good for cardiovascular health. It is recommended that women planning to conceive and those in the early stages of pregnancy have a good intake of folic acid in their diet (but supplements should also be taken to achieve the RDA at this time).

Grapefruits

Larger than oranges, grapefruits provide more juice. Their taste ranges from bitter/sour to sour/sweet. They add a mildly sour note to other sweeter juices, such as mango. Pink grapefruits are sweeter than yellow grapefruits.

Above: Vibrant pink grapefruits are sweeter than yellow ones.

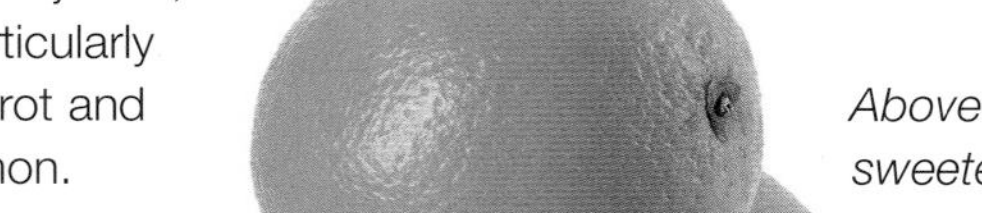

Below: Buy oranges in bulk as they make a useful base juice.

Above: Refreshing clementines work as an effective digestive cleanser.

Therapeutic uses Grapefruit juice is thought to be useful in helping to lower cholesterol. It needs to be avoided if you are taking certain medications, particularly calcium-channel blockers and some chemotherapies. Consult your medical practitioner for advice.

Lemons and Limes

These fruits have a sour/bitter taste so are used only in small quantities. They are good with tomato juice, made into lemonade or limeade, or in a hot toddy – honey and lemon juice with hot water (and brandy or whisky if you like). The delicious zesty flavour works well with almost any combination of ingredients.
Therapeutic uses Lemons have antiseptic and antibacterial properties, and are traditionally used to support liver and kidney health. They are an alkaline fruit and are often used to help calm digestive acid.

Right: Blends can be livened up with a fresh squeeze of lemon or lime juice.

Mandarins, Tangerines, Satsumas, Clementines and Tangelos

These are all different crosses of citrus fruit. They have individual mild, aromatic sweetness, which varies with the type of fruit. None of them is as tart as oranges. They make good base juices and combine well with tropical fruit.
Therapeutic uses These fruits have similar properties to oranges and are also good digestive cleansers.

Other Citrus Fruits

Kumquats These can be fairly bitter, so juice them with intensely sweet ingredients, such as apricots. Slices of kumquat may also be used to decorate glasses.

GIVE ME FIVE!
Most authorities agree that we need to eat five portions of fruit and vegetables a day, but many people are not sure what constitutes a "portion". Put simply, the daily total should come to 400g/14oz, so a portion is 80g/just under 3oz. A portion can be:
- one apple, one orange, one banana or another similar-sized fruit or vegetable
- two small fruits, such as tangerines or kiwi fruit
- half a large fruit, such as a grapefruit, or a generous slice of melon
- a small bowl of salad or fruit salad
- one cup of chopped vegetables
- one wine-glass full of fruit or vegetable juice (but remember that juice only counts towards one portion, so you can't drink juice all day and count it as five).

Note Potatoes do not count as a portion of vegetables because they are a starchy food.

Mineolas This fruit is distinguished by a bump at its stem end. It has very few pips (seeds) and is wonderfully sweet, so is perfect for juicing.
Pomelos These are a type of orange with a sharp grapefruit flavour. Their slightly dry texture renders less juice than oranges, lemons or grapefruits, but their juice makes a good addition to mixed drinks that need sharpening.
Ugli fruit Named for its appearance, this fruit is delicious, mild, acid-sweet and juicy.

Orchard and stone fruit

Apples and pears are the classic orchard fruits and they are excellent for juicing. They are available year round and are relatively cheap, making them ideal to use as base juices. Other stone and orchard fruits, such as apricots, cherries and plums, are restricted to the summer season and tend to be more expensive, but they make deliciously sweet juices. Apples and pears store well in cool, dry conditions, but it is best to keep soft fruit in the refrigerator. All of these fruits are rich in vitamins and minerals, with apricots being particularly high in betacarotene – a natural source of vitamin A.

Preparing and Juicing Orchard and Stone Fruits

To juice orchard and stone fruits, you will need either a juicer for hard fruits, such as apples and pears, or a blender or food processor for softer fruits, such as peaches or plums. You will also need a chopping board and a sharp knife. A cherry stoner is useful for removing stones (pits) from cherries.

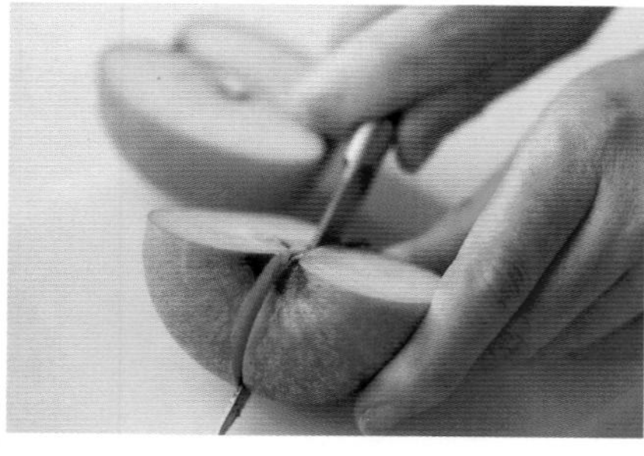

Hard fruits Apples, hard pears and quinces are best prepared with a juicer (centrifugal or masticating). Using a brush, scrub the skin with a little soap or washing-up liquid (dishwashing detergent) and water, then rinse throughly. Quarter the fruits and remove stems, but leave the core intact. Push the quarters through the juicer. Firmer peaches, nectarines or plums can also be put through a juicer, although the yield is much less than if blended. Halve or quarter these fruits and remove the stones.

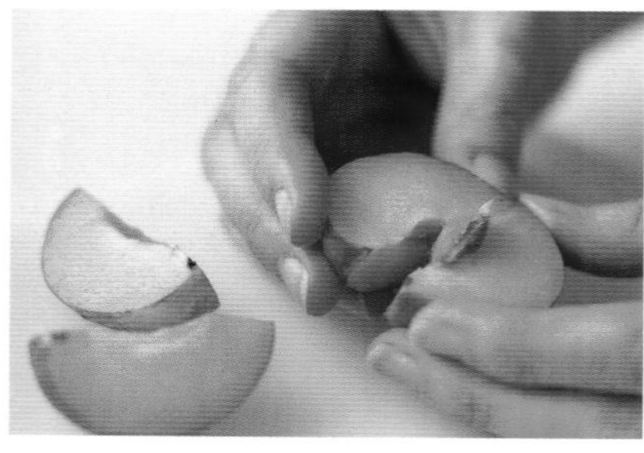

Soft fruits Ripe apricots, cherries, peaches, nectarines, plums and greengages are best prepared in a blender or food processor as they produce a deliciously thick pulp. Halve or quarter these fruits, removing the stems and stones. There is no need to peel these fruits, though leaving the peel on will give the blend a thicker texture. If you do not peel the fruit, wash it thoroughly first.

Cherries These need to be pitted and this is most easily done using a cherry pitter.

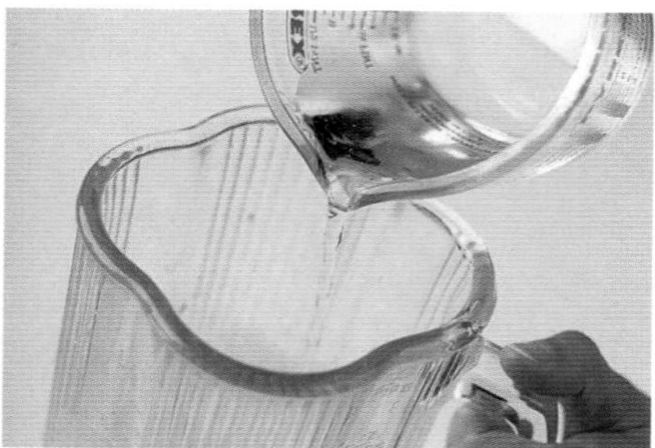

To use a blender Place the fruit in the goblet and add your choice of liquid – water or a thin fruit juice. Cover and select the appropriate speed. For a thicker consistency, add banana, avocado or another soft fruit.

To use a food processor Place the prepared fruit in the bowl, cover and secure the lid and select the appropriate speed. The resulting pulp can be diluted to drinking consistency by adding water or a liquid ingredient such as apple or orange juice. If your food processor can crush ice, add some cubes at the end to create a lovely fruit "slush" drink.

CLASSIC COMBINATIONS

In the late summer and autumn, there is often a glut of locally grown orchard fruit or berries. Buy plenty and either freeze them for use later in the year, or juice them, taking advantage of some of these classic flavour combinations.

- **Apple and blackberry** – the sweetness of the apples offsets the tart blackberries perfectly.
- **Apple and carrot** – this juice is packed full of healthy nutrients.
- **Pear, melon and ginger** – the warmth of ginger complements the cool melon in this exotic blend.
- **Peach and apricot** – this thick juice can be thinned with sparkling mineral water.
- **Nectarine and cherry** – a delicious sweet juice that children will love.
- **Pear and cranberry** – this refreshing juice should be served with plenty of crushed ice.
- **Pear and apricot** – the thick, sweet apricot juice complements the subtle, aromatic flavour of pear.

Above: Apples make juice that can be very sweet, tangy or sour.

Apples

Depending on the type of apple, the taste will range from sweet to tart or sour. For juicing purposes choose eating apples, not cooking or crab apples. Apples are available all year round, making them ideal as a base juice to which other juices can be added. Apple juice oxidizes quickly to a brown colour but a little lemon juice will slow down this process.

Some classic juice combinations are apple and cranberry, apple and blackcurrant, and apple and carrot. While it may seem that choosing sweet apples is best, sharper tasting eating varieties are often better, as juicing concentrates the sweetness. They also balance out sweeter ingredients – for instance, sharp green apples work well to counterbalance the flavour of intensely sweet watermelon.

Therapeutic uses Apples are a good all-round fruit. They contain malic acid, which aids digestion, and they are high in pectin, a soluble fibre that helps to lower cholesterol and may help in the treatment of constipation and diarrhoea. If you want to detox and generally clear out your system, apples are the perfect fruit. Some varieties are also very rich in vitamin C, so they can help to boost the immune system and stave off winter colds and flu.

Above: Aromatic pears make a subtle and refreshing juice.

Pears

These fruits have an aromatic scent and delicate flavour, which comes out particularly well when they are juiced. To fully enjoy their subtle flavour it is best not to mix them with other very strong tasting juices, although they can be used to tone down the sometimes overwhelming flavours of cabbage and celery, for example.
Therapeutic uses This is another detoxifying fruit, which also provides an energizing boost. The levulose sugar in pears is more easily tolerated by diabetics than other sugars.

Apricots

If you can, choose tree-ripened fruit as the betacarotene levels increase by 200 per cent in the final ripening period. When blended, apricots produce a thick, rich pulp that is best when diluted with other more liquid juices such as cucumber, apple or carrot. Alternatively, you could thin the juice with a splash of sparkling mineral water or add natural mineral water. Dried apricots can be soaked and prepared in a blender with some water.
Therapeutic uses Apricots are particularly rich in betacarotene, one of the most important antioxidants, while dried apricots are a useful source of iron, potassium and fibre.

Above: Apricots make a deliciously thick and nutritious juice, perfect for a healthy breakfast drink.

Above: Fresh cherries have a short season so enjoy them while you can.

Cherries

Choose ripe, sweet cherries for juicing as they do not ripen further after picking. They should be plump and firm, but not hard. Cherries lend a rich, aromatic flavour to fresh juices. Preparing them can be extremely time-consuming, and it helps if you have a cherry stoner to pit them. They are best used in small quantities combined with other flavours and they turn juices and drinks a vibrant pinky-red colour. Cherry juice combines well with most other fruits and vegetables.

Therapeutic uses Powerhouses of the phyto (plant) nutrients proanthocyanins, which derive from their red colour, cherries have potent antioxidant characteristics. They also have painkilling abilities, which some people find particularly useful for relieving rheumatism. The pain relief characteristics can also be useful for alleviating headaches – a portion of 20 cherries is reputed to be the equivalent of one aspirin in terms of painkilling ability. Fresh cherries are also traditionally used to alleviate gout by helping to moderate uric acid levels. If you cannot find fresh cherries, the canned variety make a good substitute.

Peaches and Nectarines

These fruits produce similar thick, sweet juices, with peach juice being a little sweeter than that made with nectarines – but this difference is hardly noticeable once the juice has been blended.

Peaches have a fuzzy skin, which you may prefer to peel off before juicing, but this is not necessary. It is a bit of a waste putting peaches and nectarines through a juicer as a much better yield can be achieved using a blender or food processor. This process retains the fibre of the fruit, resulting in a much thicker fruit purée, which can then be thinned if you like. If a recipe calls for fresh apricots but it is the wrong season and you cannot find them, peaches or nectarines make a good substitute.

Therapeutic uses Rich in vitamin C, betacarotene and other antioxidants, peaches and nectarines are excellent for skin, lung and digestive health, and are also particularly good for your eyes. One fresh nectarine contains an adult's entire recommended daily allowance of vitamin C. These fruits are very easy to digest but have a gentle laxative and diuretic effect, so should always be eaten in moderation.

Above: Prunes add sweet flavour to juices when whizzed up in a blender.

Above: Juice from plums can be slightly sour if the fruit is underripe.

Left: Nectarines do not need to be peeled before blending, but the large stone must be removed.

Plums, Greengages, Damsons and Prunes

Plums and greengages have a sweet, refreshing taste, although some varieties, especially if unripe, can be a little bit tart. Damsons are fairly sour with a strong flavour, so are generally cooked with sugar before using. Prunes are dried plums and are intensely sweet – they can be blended with water to make a thick sweet juice, and they combine well with most citrus fruits.

As with other sweet, soft fruit, very ripe plums and greengages are best used with other fruits that are less sweet or with more liquid ingredients, such as slightly sour apple juice. If plums are a little underripe, they will work well with extremely sweet fruits, such as bananas, mangoes, grapes or even orange juice.

Therapeutic uses Plums and prunes are known for their laxative properties. They are also very rich in potent antioxidants, making them a good choice for general health. Plums are a rich source of vitamin E and are good for maintaining healthy skin.

Quinces

These are an old-fashioned fruit but they are now becoming increasingly available throughout the year. Apple or pear-like in shape, depending on the variety, and with a pale golden colour, they have a delightful scented taste when cooked, but when eaten raw the flavour can be very astringent.

Quinces are hard when grown in cooler climates but ripen to a much softer texture when grown in warm climates. Although they are most often used in jellies and jams, for juicing purposes quinces should be prepared like apples, and are juiced in the same way. They should ideally be combined with a very sweet juice, such as peach or apricot, to counteract their tart, slightly bitter taste.

Therapeutic uses Elixir of quince was traditionally used, many years ago, to help invalids through long periods of convalescence.

Below: If you find fresh quinces, prepare them as you would apples and juice them in the same way, then combine with very sweet fruit juices such as mango or peach.

DRIED FRUITS

These are widely available and include raisins, sultanas (golden raisins) and currants, apricots, prunes, figs, mangoes, papaya, banana, apple rings and dates. Dried fruits do not juice well because they are dehydrated; however, they can be rehydrated by soaking in hot water, tea (Earl Grey is delicious), warmed wine or fortified wine. Adding cinnamon or another spice, such as cloves, complements their flavour. Dried fruits provide more concentrated sources of nutrients – including iron, magnesium and antioxidants – than their fresh equivalents. They are very sweet, so a little goes a long way in juices and drinks.

Above: Semi-dried apricots do not need soaking before use.

Above: Clockwise from top left, sultanas, currants and raisins don't juice well, but can be finely chopped and added to thicker fruit juices.

Berries and currants

Tiny delicious currants and ripe berries are ideal for thicker juices. You will need a blender or a food processor for this because soft fruits do not go through juicers as successfully as hard fruits. Berries are mainly a summer fruit and this is when they not only taste their best but are also cheapest, although they are often imported at other times of the year. They must be stored in the refrigerator and are best used within two days of purchase. Berries need careful handling and you need to watch them as they can quickly become overripe. If you cannot find fresh berries and currants, frozen ones are a good option.

Weight for weight, strawberries, raspberries and blackcurrants contain as much vitamin C as citrus fruits. Dark red berries are also rich sources of proanthocyanins, which are powerful antioxidants. Some people have an allergic reaction to strawberries and other berries, especially if they eat too many, and this can result in a strawberry rash or even a fever.

FREEZING FRUIT
If there is a glut of berries you can freeze them for juicing at other times of the year.

Remove the stalks and leaves, then place the fruit on a baking sheet in a single layer to freeze. Once frozen transfer to a freezerproof container or bag. When you want to use them, either defrost first or blend from frozen for an iced effect.

Preparing and Blending Berries and Currants

To juice berries and currants, you will need either a blender or a food processor, a chopping board and a small, sharp knife.

Soft fruits These are easy to prepare for blending. Rinse, then discard any overripe or mouldy fruit. Remove any stems and leaves, either pulling them off by hand or using a sharp knife. Remove the calyx from strawberries, but remember there is no need to hull them when making juices.

To use a blender Place the prepared soft fruits in the flask, add liquid, such as mineral water or fresh fruit juice, cover securely with the lid and select the appropriate speed. You can add banana or other soft fruits to make a thicker consistency.

To use a food processor Place the prepared fruit in the bowl, cover and process. If you prefer a thinner consistency, the resulting pulp can be diluted by adding mineral water (still or sparkling, depending on your preference), or a liquid juice such as orange or apple juice.

Adding ice Create a delicious berry ice crush by adding plenty of ice to the blend. Before crushing ice in a blender of food processor, however, check the manufacturer's instructions.

MAKING A FRUIT COULIS
Coulis make delicious, jewel-coloured additions to trickle over an ice cream or dessert before serving.

1 Choose one fruit depending on the colour or flavour you want: raspberries or strawberries for dark red or pinkish red, peeled kiwi fruit for bright green or soaked dried apricots for a vibrant orange colour.

2 Put the fruit in a blender – approximately one small handful per person should be enough. Blend on high speed until puréed. If using dried apricots you will need to add 15–30ml/1–2 tbsp water before blending to achieve the correct consistency.

3 Strain the raspberry or strawberry coulis if you want a seedless purée.

Above: Buy plenty of strawberries for juicing when they are in season.

Strawberries, Raspberries, Blackberries and Mulberries

Generally sweet but with a sharp undertone, strawberries are at their best and sweetest when perfectly ripe. Wild strawberries are much smaller than cultivated strawberries and have an intense, delicious flavour, but they are generally too expensive to blend into fresh juices unless you are lucky enough to have your own supply. Buy brightly coloured, plump strawberries and do not wash them until just before you are ready to use them.

Raspberries are a delicate berry so handle them with great care, giving them just a light rinse, if necessary. They are more tart tasting than strawberries and they add a deeper reddish colour to juices whereas strawberries give a light pinky colour to a drink. Try combining raspberry with peach juice.

Blackberries arrive later in the summer season than other berries, usually just as autumn is approaching. They grow wild in the countryside in abundance so you could easily pick your own batch, but you can also find cultivated blackberries in large supermarkets. They are very sweet and juicy when fully ripe.

Mulberries look a bit like blackberries in size and shape but they are less widely available. When ripe, their flavour is sweet but slightly sour and they are less aromatic than other berries.

When in season these fruits will be reasonably priced and you could use them as a base juice, but at other times, when the fruit is more expensive, just a few berries will add a really distinctive taste and colour to drinks. They blend well with bananas, orange juice, apples, melons, peaches and most other delicately flavoured fruits. Blackberries will dominate the colour of most other juices, turning the blend a deep, dark purple, but the taste is subtle enough to mix well with most fruit and vegetable combinations. Blackberries go particularly well with apples – a classic combination.

Therapeutic uses Strawberries are rich in pectin and ellagic acid, which makes them excellent for cleansing and detoxification. All four berries are good sources of proanthocyanins and have lots of vitamin C, both of which are good for boosting the immune system. As an antioxidant, vitamin C may even reduce the risk of developing certain cancers. Berries are a valuable source of calcium, which is important for healthy bones and teeth, and they are also soothing for the nervous system. People with cardiovascular health problems should include berries in their diet for their antioxidant properties. Raspberry juice is believed to cleanse the digestive system, and raspberries have traditionally been used in the treatment of diarrhoea, indigestion and rheumatism.

Above: Raspberries add a delicious tart flavour and a vibrant red colour.

Right: Hunt for wild blackberry bushes, then pick your own.

Above: The intense colour of blueberries will dominate any blend you add them to.

Blueberries

Blueberries are very sweet when ripe, but rather tart when underripe. Generally, they have a short summer season, though in warm countries the season is prolonged. Buy plenty and freeze them in small bags.

As with blackberries, the dark colour of blueberries will dominate the blend; in this case the juice is a rich bluish-purple. They are a delicious addition to most fruit blends or, if you prefer simple juices, just add sparkling mineral water to a thick blueberry purée.

Therapeutic uses Blueberries are one of the most potent fruits in terms of antioxidant power. Primarily used to boost the immune system, they also play an important role in eye health. During World War II, pilots ate blueberries because they believed it would improve their night vision. As with cranberries, they are good for relieving urinary tract infections.

Blackcurrants, Redcurrants and Whitecurrants

The general flavour of blackcurrants is sour-sweet, depending on how ripe they are. They are best sweetened, although this is not necessary if you are mixing a small amount of blackcurrant juice with a sweeter fruit juice. They make ideal mixers but they are not good juiced on their own. Blackcurrants are more often made into cordials (non-alcoholic) than into juices, and you could add some cordial to a juice made of other fruits.

Redcurrants and whitecurrants are available at the same time of the year as blackcurrants but are less abundant and can be more difficult to find. They are good mixed with less expensive blackcurrants.

Therapeutic uses Few fruits and vegetables have more vitamin C than blackcurrants, making them powerful allies in wintertime for fending off colds and flu. Blackcurrant seeds are a rich source of essential fatty acids (the same as those in evening primrose oil), which are helpful for female hormonal health, relieving symptoms of pre-menstrual syndrome and mastalgia (sore breasts).

Left: Whitecurrants are sweeter than other currants and less tart.

Left: Mix redcurrants with sweeter ingredients for a delicious juice.

Above: Tart blackcurrants contain more vitamin C than almost any other fruit, but are best used in small quantities.

Above: Cranberries mix well with sweet orchard fruits, such as pears.

Cranberries

These lovely berries are associated with the winter season as they are generally not available fresh at other times of the year. Buy them when available and keep them in your freezer until needed. Cranberries are fairly sour and need to be sweetened. They work well with juice made from sweet oranges, apples, pears or carrots in a ratio of a quarter cranberry juice to three-quarters of the sweeter ingredient.
Therapeutic uses Cranberries are very successful at preventing or resolving cystitis and other urinary tract infections when drunk as a juice over several days. The antioxidants they contain specifically target the bacteria of the urinary tract and prevent them from adhering and causing damage. The quinine contained in cranberries is an effective liver detoxifier.

Other Berries

Elderberries These are not generally available to buy but must be gathered from the tree. The elder tree grows widely in the countryside and can also be found in many urban gardens, as well as on waste ground. The berry is too tiny and sour for juicing, but makes an excellent sweet syrup when boiled with sugar and water. Elderflower syrup is a traditional immune-boosting drink. In spring and early summer, the flowers are gathered and can be used to make delicious and fragrant elderflower cordial.

Gooseberries These have a short summer season but can be frozen on baking sheets. They are widely available but not often used for juicing because they can be extremely sour. However, you could add a small number to a juice to gain the benefit of their immune-supporting effects.

Below: Instead of juicing raw, elderberries are boiled with sugar to make a syrup.

SUMMER JUICE BLENDS

When there is a glut of surplus berries but you don't want to freeze them, try making some of these classic berry juices.

- **Raspberry and orange** – this has a delicious tart flavour and is perfect for breakfast.
- **Cranberry and pear** – sweet and juicy pear contrasts with the slightly dry flavour of cranberries.
- **Summer fruits** – simply redcurrants, raspberries, strawberries and blackberries.
- **Redcurrant and cranberry** – a tart and refreshing juice, perfect on a summer's day.
- **Raspberry and apple** – kids will love this combination with plenty of crushed ice.
- **Blueberry and orange** – this drink will take on a vibrant bluish-purple colour.
- **Blackberry and cinnamon** – a warm, spicy drink guaranteed to impress guests.

Left: Freeze gooseberries to use all year round.

Exotic and other fruits

Most exotic fruits are now available year round. These fruits are best blended because, apart from melons and pineapples, they will not go through a juicer very well. Melons, pineapples and bananas produce enough juice to use as base ingredients, but the availability and yield of other exotic fruits mean that they are best used in smaller quantities. Orange-coloured fruits, such as mangoes, are excellent sources of betacarotene.

Preparing and Juicing Exotic and Other Fruits

You will need a blender or food processor, a juicer (centrifugal or masticating), a chopping board and a sharp knife. A spoon is useful for scooping the flesh out of some fruits.

Melons Cut a wedge and scoop out the pips (seeds). Cut away the flesh and purée in a blender or food processor. Firmer melons can be put through a juicer, particularly watermelon.

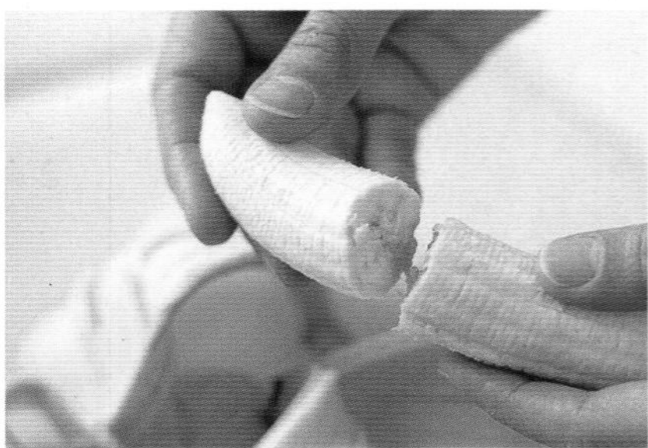

Bananas Peel and then break the flesh into chunks. Put the banana into a blender or food processor and blend to a pulp, then add other fruit juice until you get the desired consistency.

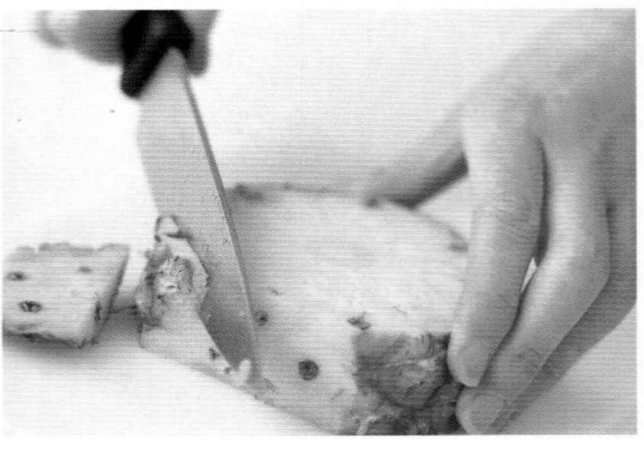

Pineapples Lay the pineapple on its side on a chopping board, then, using a large sharp knife, slice off the base and the top. Cut the fruit into thick slices, then remove the skin. The flesh can be put in a blender or food processor, or pushed through a juicer.

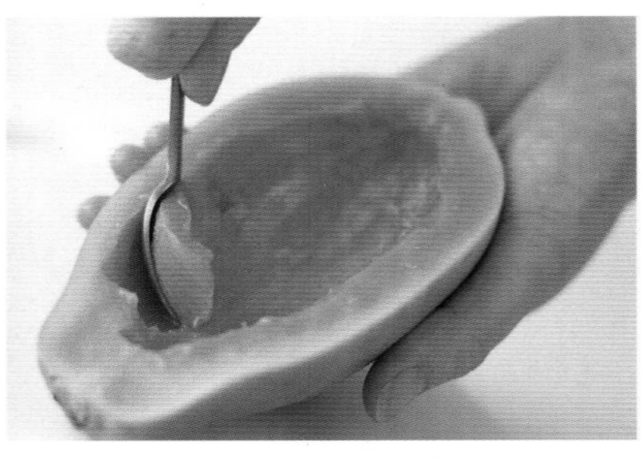

Kiwi fruit, papayas and guavas Cut the fruit in half. For papayas and guavas, scoop out the seeds. For all three fruits, either scoop out the ripe flesh with a spoon or peel with a sharp knife. Put the flesh in a blender or food processor. None of these yields enough juice when put through a juicer.

Mangoes Peel the fruit and cut the flesh away from either side of the stone (pit). Then remove as much flesh as possible away from the stone (pit) and into a blender or food processor.

Lychees The easiest way to peel lychees is by hand; the skin is stiff and cracks easily. Ease the fruit out and remove the stone (pit). Put the flesh in a blender or food processor. Lychees do not yield enough juice in a juicer.

RHUBARB

Traces of oxalic acid, which inhibits calcium and iron absorption and may exacerbate joint problems, can be found in many vegetables. The high levels of oxalic acid in rhubarb mean that it should not be used raw, and rhubarb leaves should never be eaten because they are poisonous. Rhubarb can, however, be added to drinks if it is cooked first. It contains high levels of calcium, potassium and thiamine (vitamin B_1).

Right: Add bananas to drinks for a thick, creamy texture.

Bananas

Once an exotic fruit, bananas are now a staple. Smaller and much more flavourful bananas are becoming generally available and they are well worth buying.

Bananas are excellent for thickening thin fruit juices and combine well with many different fruits, although they are not good when partnered with vegetables. They are a great addition to a blend and make it more filling, especially if you want a breakfast time boost.

Therapeutic uses
Bananas are very good energy boosters and they are full of bowel-supporting, gentle fibre.

Pineapples

These are sweet to sweet-sharp tasting, often with an aromatic note. Pineapples do not ripen further once harvested, so make sure you buy a fruit that is ripe. Select a pineapple that is slightly soft to the touch, smells delicious and has a good colour with no green patches. The leaves should be crisp and green, with no sign of yellowing at the tips. Pineapple combines extremely well with most fruits and also with vegetable juices.

Therapeutic uses Fresh pineapples contain one of the strongest protein-digesting enzymes, bromelain, making them valuable for all digestive complaints. They even "tidy up" the digestive tract by skimming off dead cells, and they can help to heal damaged digestive tracts.

The enzymes also help to clear the blood and break down clots. Pineapple is thought to relieve arthritis and may help to reduce back pain. This fruit also helps to get rid of mucus build-up.

Kiwi Fruit

Like the banana, kiwi fruit was once exotic but is now very easy to buy. If kiwi fruit are hard when bought they will ripen quickly on a windowsill. They taste sweet, zesty and aromatic when ripe and are inexpensive enough to use as a base juice. They combine well with other green fruits, such as apples or grapes, as well as tropical fruits.

Therapeutic uses Kiwi fruit is one of the richest sources of immune-boosting and collagen-building vitamin C.

Above: Kiwi fruit make a delicious, tangy base juice.

Above: Pineapples can be mixed with most fruits.

Left: Ripe mangoes have extremely soft flesh that is juicy and sweet.

Mangoes, Papayas and Guavas

These fruits are best bought ripe, when they yield slightly to gentle pressure, which is when they are at their sweetest. They are all aromatic, delicious and luxurious tasting. They combine well with bananas, oranges, apples or carrots to make tasty tropical drinks.

Therapeutic uses Papaya is distinguished by its potent digestive enzyme, papain, which has all the advantages of bromelain (see pineapples). Papain also has a reputation for helping to restore healthy bowel flora (bacterial balance). All three fruits are rich in betacarotene and contain generous amounts of vitamin C as well as many minerals, making them excellent all-round sources of nutrition.

Lychees

Lychees have a subtle, aromatic and sweet taste. They need to be combined with equally delicately flavoured fruits so that their subtle flavour is not lost. Combine them in a drink with melons, bananas, apples or strawberries.

Therapeutic uses Lychees are a good source of vitamin C.

Right: The juice from Galia melons is delicious when combined with either fruit or vegetables.

Melons

There are many different types of melon available, including cantaloupe, honeydew and watermelon. They are members of the gourd family, which also includes cucumbers and squashes. To choose a ripe melon (apart from watermelon), press the blossom end, which should yield slightly to gentle pressure. A ripe melon will have a sweet, perfumed aroma. For watermelon, tap the side of the fruit, which should sound hollow; the rind should barely give when pressed with a thumb.

Melons make a sweet, refreshing base juice that combines well with other fruits, such as tart apples or pears, or with slightly bitter vegetables such as cabbage.

Above: Aromatic lychees contain significant amounts of vitamin C.

Therapeutic uses Melons have a diuretic and digestive cleansing action, and they are good for all problem skin conditions. The seeds are very rich in potassium, which helps to lower high blood pressure, and they are also valued for their zinc and vitamin E content, so it is worthwhile including a few. All of the orange-fleshed melons are rich in betacarotene, which is good for the immune system and for eye health in general. Watermelon also provides the phytonutrient lycopene, which is reputedly powerful in fighting against certain types of cancer, including prostate cancer. Lycopene must be consumed together with a small amount of fat to facilitate absorption, and supplements are recommended to gain its full benefit.

Grapes

Depending on the variety, grapes can be sweet or tart tasting. Black, red and green (or "white") grapes are available, and you can choose from seeded or seedless varieties. They produce a light green or pink juice depending on the colour of the grape.

Grapes are fairly watery so they work well with fruits that produce thicker juice, such as mangoes, papayas, peaches or plums. They are a useful and delicious addition to most fruit and vegetable juices.

Therapeutic uses Dark-skinned grapes are rich in a compound called resveratrol, one of the most potent antioxidants, as well as proanthocyanins, and all colours of grapes have high levels of ellagic acid, which is a potent detoxifier. Grape juice is a traditional naturopathic rest cure and is also sometimes used as a nerve tonic. Grapes have been reported to help alleviate the symptoms of arthritis.

Right: There is no need to remove grape seeds before blending as they will just be incorporated into the juice.

TROPICAL TOPPERS

Whilst some tropical fruits do not yield much juice, or are fiddly to prepare, they can be ideal for making elegant and exotic decorations and toppings.

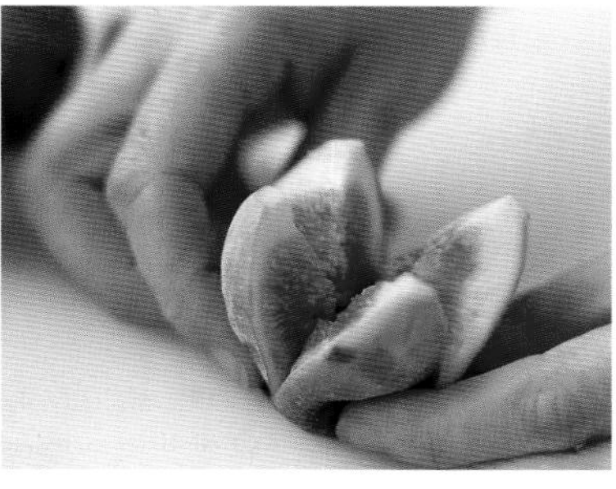

Figs Cut from the pointed end downwards but do not cut right through the base. Make a second cut at right angles to the first, creating a cross shape. Squeeze the fruit gently to open up into a "flower". This makes an attractive edible decoration – eat them with the skin on. Figs do not yield much juice but you can combine them with other juices. They have a strong laxative action, so should be consumed in moderation, and are useful for irritated bronchial tubes.

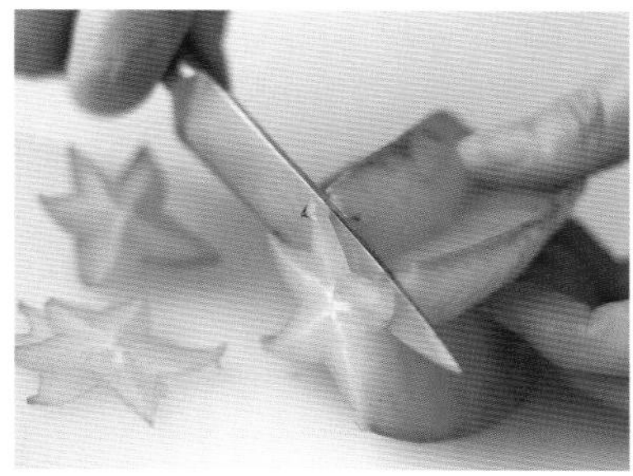

Star fruit (carambola) These pretty tropical fruits can be sliced very thinly into attractive star-shaped decorations.

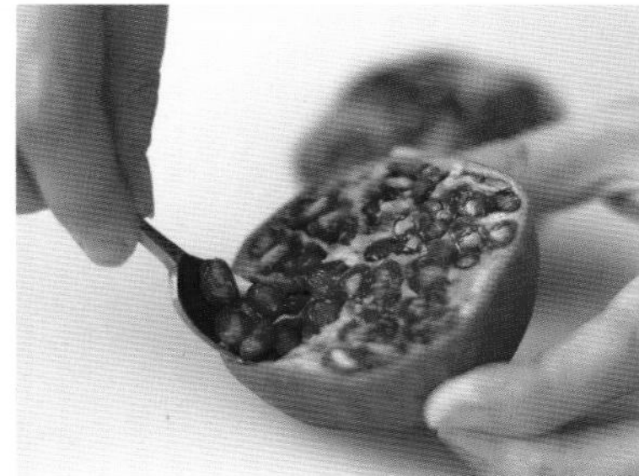

Pomegranates Cut these in half and scoop out the scarlet pips (seeds), separating them from the pith. Sweet, refreshing and crunchy, the pips are ideal for sprinkling on top of juices.

Passion fruit Cut in half and scoop out the pulp and pips (seeds). Sweet, aromatic and attractive, this pulp makes an ideal juice topping.

Dates Cut dates in half and discard the stone (pit). Although they cannot be juiced, they can be chopped and added to blends. Otherwise, slice thinly and serve as a side snack with a drink.

Root and tuber vegetables

These vegetables must be juiced using a centrifugal or masticating juicer. Carrot is the only root vegetable that is suitable to be used as a base juice, but others can be included in smaller proportions in juices and blends. Root vegetables are essentially autumnal and winter vegetables, but they are generally available year round. They all store best in cool, dry conditions, although beetroot (beet) is best kept in the refrigerator.

Preparing and Juicing Root and Tuber Vegetables

To juice root and tuber vegetables, you will need an electric juicer (centrifugal or masticating), a scrubbing brush or a vegetable peeler, a chopping board and a sharp knife.

Peeling When preparing root and tuber vegetables, decide first if you are going to peel them or just scrub off the dirt. With many fruits and vegetables it is a shame to peel them as a good proportion of the nutrients are just under the skin. Your decision will be, in part, influenced by how thin the skin is. You may want to peel old and gnarled carrots but leave small new carrots unpeeled. You do not usually need to peel carrots, beetroot (beets), celeriac, parsnips, radishes, swedes (rutabagas), turnips, sweet potatoes or yams. While you can include potato skin, you must be sure to cut away any peel or flesh that is sprouting or green in any way. This green colour indicates the presence of a highly toxic alkaloid called solanine, which could cause illness.

Juicing When root vegetables are juiced they tend to produce foam, which settles at the top of the juice. This can taste a bit earthy (even when the vegetables have been scrubbed clean). However, this taste indicates their high mineral content so the topping should be drunk for maximum benefit (you can mix it in with the rest of the juice). If you find the taste particularly unpleasant, just spoon it off, but do not strain the juice.

Carrots

When juiced, carrots are very sweet and the fresh juice has a much better flavour than commercial carrot juice. Because they yield a lot of mild-tasting juice, carrots provide the basis for many combinations. They work very well with both vegetables and fruit.

Therapeutic uses Rich in betacarotene, which is good for the immune system as well as for skin and eye health.

Nursing mothers are sometimes advised to drink carrot juice; it contains more easily assimilated calcium than cow's milk, which is essential to healthy growth in infancy. To ensure that betacarotene is converted to vitamin A (a fat-soluble vitamin) as needed, it helps to add 5ml/1 tsp flax seed oil or walnut oil to the carrot juice, or some full cream (whole) or semi-skimmed (low-fat) milk.

Beetroot

A rich ruby-red colour is imparted to drinks by the inclusion of beetroot (beets). Always used raw, they do not need to be peeled, just scrubbed. The juice is quite strong tasting, so use it sparingly: about one-quarter beetroot juice to three-quarters other juice.

Beetroot greens enhance the nutritional value of the juice. However, they are fairly high in oxalic acid, which is poisonous if consumed in large quantities. Juiced beetroot and leaves work well in all vegetable combinations.

Therapeutic uses Beetroot is used as a blood fortifier and iron builder in traditional herbalism, particularly for heavy menstrual blood loss. It is very rich in immune-boosting beta-carotene, as well as many other minerals, including iron and manganese. It is also traditionally used during convalescence.

Above: Carrots make a sweet juice that works well as a base when combined with juice from other fruits or vegetables.

Right: Beetroot provides a stunning deep red juice.

Parsnips

This vegetable is high in sugar and so, like carrots, tastes fairly sweet. The juice is also quite creamy tasting. However, unlike carrot juice, parsnip juice should be added in smaller quantities – about one-quarter parsnip to three-quarters other juice. It works best with other vegetable juices, especially slightly spicy, peppery ones.

Therapeutic uses Parsnips have a settling effect on the stomach and are mildly diuretic. Rich in silicon, they are also good for hair, skin and nails.

Radishes

These attractive vegetables come in a variety of shapes and sizes. They have a distinctive peppery taste, so use them in small quantities as a flavouring for other vegetable juices. They are ideal for bringing a bland juice to life.

Therapeutic uses As with any peppery vegetable, radishes have a tonic effect on the liver and gall bladder. They also help to clear the sinuses.

Sweet Potatoes and Yams

Although these two vegetables look similar, they are not actually related and yams tend to be drier than sweet potatoes. There are many varieties of sweet potato, with flesh ranging from pale yellow to a vivid orange. Yam flesh varies from off-white, to yellow and pink, or even purple. Choose unblemished, smooth produce and store in a dark, cool, dry place.

Above: Peppery radishes should be juiced in small quantities only.

Therapeutic uses Both of these tubers are high in starch, with yams containing more natural sugar then sweet potatoes, but with a lower vitamin A and C content. They are both energizing and easier to digest than standard potatoes and they have an alkalizing effect on the body, which helps to curb over-acidity. Some people believe that they have anti-carcinogenic properties.

Celeriac, Swedes and Turnips

Celeriac has a mild celery taste; swede (rutabaga) is sweet and creamy but slightly earthy tasting; and turnips taste mild and peppery. Most of the nutrients in turnips are concentrated in the tops, so juice them along with the stems and leaves instead of discarding them. All of these vegetables work best when added to other vegetable blends, for example in a carrot-based juice with green leafy vegetables, but they do not combine particularly well with fruit.

Therapeutic uses Celeriac has a mildly astringent, diuretic action, while swede is energizing. Turnips, with their tops, provide a good source of calcium (without the limiting oxalic acid found in beetroot (beet) and spinach), making them a good nerve tonic, and they are also thought to be useful when you are feeling run down or depressed. By weight, turnip tops contain twice as much vitamin C as citrus fruit, and they also have an expectorant action, which is useful for chesty coughs.

Potatoes

Any type of potato can be used, but you must always use them raw in blended drinks. Potato is not a juice that anybody would drink on its own, but it has a slightly nutty flavour that is not unpleasant when mixed with other vegetable juices. It does, however, have good therapeutic effects, which makes it worth including. You only need a small quantity mixed with another juice, such as carrot, at a ratio of about one-eighth potato to seven-eighths other juice. (See the important note about preparation of potatoes opposite.)

Therapeutic uses Potato peel is high in potassium and may help to lower blood pressure, while the juice has traditionally been used to treat stomach ulcers and arthritis.

Above: The juice from potatoes is added to drinks for its therapeutic effect.

Leafy and brassica vegetables

Green leafy vegetables and brassicas need to be juiced using a juicer. The brassica family includes broccoli, cauliflower and Brussels sprouts. Ideally these, and all leafy vegetables, should be stored in the refrigerator to avoid wilting, yellowing or browning, and they are best used as soon as possible after purchase as they quickly lose their nutritional value. They are all used in small quantities, to add flavour or for their nutritional or therapeutic properties, with other bulkier base juices. Generally you will add one-quarter juice made from green leaves to three-quarters juice made from other ingredients.

All dark green leafy vegetables are good sources of magnesium and betacarotene, and many are also rich in iron. This group has important health qualities. They are all rich in compounds such as sulphurophanes, which are responsible for the vegetables' slightly bitter taste, and indole-3-carbinol, which is believed to have cancer-inhibiting properties.

Preparing and Juicing Leafy and Brassica Vegetables

To juice leafy and brassica vegetables, you will need a juicer (centrifugal or masticating), a chopping board and a sharp knife.

Loose, leafy vegetables Separate out the leaves and wash thoroughly. Cut away any that are discoloured but keep the outer leaves as they are richer in nutrients than the interior ones. Do not discard the cores of lettuce or any leaf stems.

Tightly packed leaves Vegetables such as chicory (Belgian endive) or Chinese leaves (Chinese cabbage) should be washed, then quartered or chopped into an appropriate size to pass through the neck of the machine. Cut broccoli and cauliflower into florets and wash the pieces thoroughly. The cores can also be juiced.

To extract the maximum juice It is best to alternate putting leaves through the machine with a hard vegetable or fruit such as carrot or apple. This keeps the machine working efficiently to extract the maximum juice.

Cabbages and Brussels Sprouts

Dark green cabbage is the best choice for juicing as it is nutrient-rich. White cabbage is its poor relation, nutritionally speaking. Red cabbage generally tastes better when cooked, but if it is used for juicing the lovely purple colour will dominate your blend. Cabbage lends a surprisingly light, green taste to juices as long as the quantity of cabbage used does not overwhelm the blend. About one-eighth to one-quarter cabbage is the right quantity in any juice. Brussels sprouts, taste similar to cabbages when juiced but are slightly more nutty. The leafy tops are also good when they are available.

Therapeutic uses Using the dark green, outer leaves is important if you want to obtain the maximum level of nutrients. Along with the rest of the brassica family, cabbages are regarded as anti-cancer vegetables. Cabbage juice is also a powerful gut and ulcer healer. It should not be used excessively by people with underactive thyroids because cabbages are known to be goitrogenous and interfere with thyroid function.

These and other leafy vegetables should also be eaten in moderation by people on blood-thinning medication, as they are high in the blood-clotting factor, vitamin K. Cabbages and Brussels sprouts provide the richest vegetable sources of vitamin C.

Spinach

This has a mild, slightly peppery taste and lends a delightful green colour to juices. It is used in small quantities to add taste and nutrients to other sweeter bases, including some milder fruits such as apples or pears.

Therapeutic uses Spinach is very nutritious, high in betacarotene and folic acid, and rich in vitamins A and C. Its iron content is good although not as high as was once believed. It also contains the phytochemicals xeaxanthin and lutein, which are known to protect the eyes against ageing.

Above: Brussels sprouts should be juiced in small quantities only.

Above: Known as a superfood, broccoli is packed with iron and vitamin C.

Cauliflower and Broccoli

These vegetables should have tightly packed, firm heads, showing no signs of wilt or discoloration. They are both available in more exotic forms, such as purple sprouting broccoli and cauliflower hybrids, and these can also be juiced, although these varieties can be expensive. Broccoli tastes slightly bitter while cauliflower is creamy. They are best used in small quantities with other milder flavours such as carrot or beetroot (beet).

Therapeutic uses Along with cabbage and Brussels sprouts, these are thought to be anti-cancer foods, and they are powerful additions to juices. They are not goitrogenous but are high in vitamin K. Broccoli is a good source of vitamin C.

Lettuce

There are many types of lettuce available. It is easier to juice firm rather than softer leaves. Most varieties lend a slightly bitter taste to juices, so should only be used in small quantities. It works well in either vegetable or fruit blends.

Therapeutic uses Lettuce is well known for its soporific, calming and sleep-inducing qualities. Very rich in asparagine, which is also found in asparagus, it has a slight laxative and digestive cleansing effect.

Kale and Watercress

Both of these vegetables are strong tasting; kale is slightly bitter while watercress has a peppery flavour, so add only small amounts to juices. They are best used alongside other vegetable juices.

Therapeutic uses Watercress and kale are nutrient powerhouses, and are used extensively in therapeutic juicing. Excellent sources of magnesium, calcium and iron, watercress is also rich in sulphur, which is good for the hair and nails.

Other Leafy Vegetables

There are many different types of leafy vegetables. Slightly bitter or peppery leaves include radicchio, rocket (arugula), Swiss chard, chicory (Belgian endive) and endive (US chicory). These are best when used in small quantities and mixed with other vegetable juices. Sweeter tasting leaves include Chinese leaves (Chinese cabbage) and pak choi (bok choy) – these combine well with both vegetable and fruit juices.

Above: All green-leafed vegetables are full of minerals and nutrients but should be mixed with other vegetables.

SUPERTASTERS

It has been identified that at least one-quarter of people are "supertasters" and have a very acute sense of taste, particularly for bitter and sour flavours. These people find that foods such as grapefruit, broccoli and Brussels sprouts are so bitter that they are unpleasant.

The result is that "supertasters" eat fewer vegetables to the point where it might impact on their health. Juicing is ideal for this group, as bitter tastes can be masked by sweeter and milder flavours from healthy sources.

Therapeutic uses Leaves are excellent sources of minerals, and darker ones contain lots of carotenoids, which help to neutralize free radicals. Bitter-tasting leaves contain chemicals that are thought to have liver, gall bladder and digestive cleansing properties.

Wild Greens

Look around when you are out on a walk and you will be able to identify a number of wild greens. In times gone by everyone was familiar with these free foods and they were incorporated into many dishes. It is fairly easy to find dandelion, sorrel and nettles, and watercress can also be found in some areas. Before gathering these plants make sure you have identified them correctly and check that they have not been sprayed with weed killers.

Therapeutic uses Wild greens are traditionally used in tonics to cure anaemia. Dandelion leaves are used as a nerve tonic and also help to balance acid/alkaline levels, which makes them useful in arthritic conditions. Nettles are believed to be useful in combating the symptoms of hay fever, and they are also thought to be helpful in relieving rheumatism and settling nervous eczema.

Vegetable fruits

Some vegetables are actually the fruit of the plant, although they are not sweet in the way that we usually think of fruit. If allowed to ripen on the plant they are all exceptionally rich in various nutrients.

Preparing and Juicing Vegetable Fruits

You will need a chopping board, a sharp knife, a spoon, a fork, a blender or food processor and a juicer (masticating or centrifugal).

Preparing avocados Make sure the avocado is ripe and yields slightly to pressure applied to the skin. Cut the avocado in half lengthways, ease the two halves apart and scoop out the stone (pit) with a spoon. Scoop out the flesh and place it in a blender or food processor with other ingredients. (Avocados are too soft to put in a juicer.)

You could also mash the flesh using a fork and stir it into a blend by hand.

Juicing peppers Cut the pepper in half lengthways, then cut away the stem, seeds and pith. Wash under running water to remove any remaining seeds, then push the flesh through a juicer.

Skinning tomatoes These can be juiced whole or skinned first. To skin tomatoes, place them in a heatproof bowl and pour boiling water over them. Leave to soak for 2–3 minutes. Lift the tomatoes out, nick the skin with the point of a knife and it should begin to peel back. Peel off the loosened skin. Blend the tomatoes in a blender or food processor.

Avocados

When properly ripe, avocados are rich and slightly nutty tasting. They lend a creamy texture to juices and can be used to thicken a thinner juice blend. They combine well with most vegetable juices – adding a little lemon or lime juice will help cut through the richness and will slow down discoloration.

Therapeutic uses Avocados are an excellent source of oleic acid, which is associated with heart health. They are also full of vitamin E, which is essential for healthy skin.

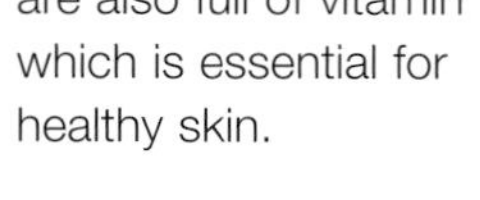

Peppers

Although they come in a variety of colours, (bell) peppers are all the same vegetable – green peppers are simply unripe red peppers. Peppers do not ripen much after picking, so they don't change colour or become sweeter. The taste of yellow, orange and red peppers is similarly sweet, while green ones have a slightly more bitter flavour.

Peppers can dominate a juice and so are best used in small quantities. They are ideal combined with tomato juice.

Therapeutic uses Peppers are one of the richest sources of vitamin C, so they provide support for the immune system. Yellow, orange and red peppers also contain high levels of the antioxidant betacarotene.

Below: Avocados contain plenty of vitamin E, making them good for the skin.

Tomatoes

Mild-tasting tomatoes are sweet when ripe and acidic when unripe. Select vine-ripened tomatoes for the best flavour. Tomatoes mix well with most other vegetables and fruits. They are often used as a base juice as they are abundant and versatile.

Therapeutic uses Tomatoes are a rich source of lycopene, which has stronger antioxidant properties than betacarotene. They are also thought to have anti-cancer properties.

Left: For the best flavour, store tomatoes at room temperature.

Squash vegetables

The high water content of these vegetables makes them ideal for juicing in a centrifugal or masticating juicer. Cucumbers are available all year round and the best variety to use for juicing is the English (hothouse) cucumber. Courgettes (zucchini) are also available all year round, but are at their best in the summer, and other squashes only appear in the autumn. Cucumbers and courgettes should be stored in the refrigerator, but other squashes may be kept for up to a week or two in cool, dry conditions.

Preparing and Juicing Squash Vegetables

To juice squash vegetables, you will need a juicer (either centrifugal or masticating), a clean chopping board and a sharp knife.

Preparing cucumbers and courgettes Wash the skin, using a scrubbing brush if the vegetables are waxed. There is no need to peel or seed them, but do so if you prefer. Cut into large chunks and push through the juicer. You could also blend cucumbers in a blender or food processor as they contain so much water.

Right: Courgette skin contains valuable nutrients so don't peel before juicing.

Juicing squashes Cut large squashes, such as butternut and pumpkin, in half and scoop out most of the seeds, leaving some to go through the juicer, if you like. Slice away the peel, then cut the flesh into large chunks and push through the juicer.

Cucumbers and Courgettes

When juiced, all cucumbers are mild and tasty, although small cucumbers have the best flavour. Ideal for using as a base juice, they mix well with both vegetables and fruit. Courgettes (zucchini) are similar to cucumbers when juiced, but not quite as sweet.
Therapeutic uses The nutrients of cucumbers and courgettes are mainly concentrated in the skin, which is why you should leave it on. If this is too bitter, experiment with peeling half the skin. These vegetables have a strong diuretic action and help to lower high blood pressure. They support healthy hair and nail growth, and also help relieve the symptoms of rheumatism.

JUICY SOUP

Raw vegetable juices can be used very successfully as soups. Either enjoy them cold in the summer, garnished with a dollop of cream or yogurt and chopped fresh herbs, or warm them through (but do not boil) in the winter months.

Gazpacho, which is made with raw tomatoes, cucumber and (bell) peppers, is the classic soup made in this way.

Pumpkins and Butternut Squash

Both of these squashes produce a juice with a surprisingly sweet and nutty taste, but it is not a juice that you would want to drink on its own. Mix one-quarter pumpkin or squash juice with three-quarters other vegetable juice, such as carrot or cucumber, along with something else to give it a bit of a zing – perhaps a bit of onion.
Therapeutic uses Be sure to include some of the seeds in the juice as they are high in zinc and iron. As with all the vegetables in this family they have a kidney-supporting and anti-water-retention action and are also powerhouses of carotenoid antioxidants.

Above: Pumpkins produce a sweet, nutty juice that is best mixed with other flavours.

Pod, shoot and bulb vegetables

All of these vegetables need to be put through a juicer. They all produce fairly strong tasting juices which should be combined with other vegetables. Pods and bulbs share the common trait that they, along with seeds, are potential plants. This means that all the goodness for the growing plant is stored in the pod or bulb ready for use, so you get many extra nutritional benefits. Shoots are also highly nutritious because they are at the stage of growth before a fully-fledged plant develops – they are fantastically rich in nutritional power for the growing plant.

Preparing and Juicing Pod, Shoot and Bulb Vegetables

To juice pod, shoot and bulb vegetables, you will need a juicer (centrifugal or masticating), a chopping board and a sharp knife.

Preparing pods French (green) beans, broad (fava) beans, runner beans and mangetouts (snow peas) do not need any preparation other than ensuring that they are clean. They do not require stringing or trimming as the juicer will simply turn the undesirable parts of the vegetables into pulp.

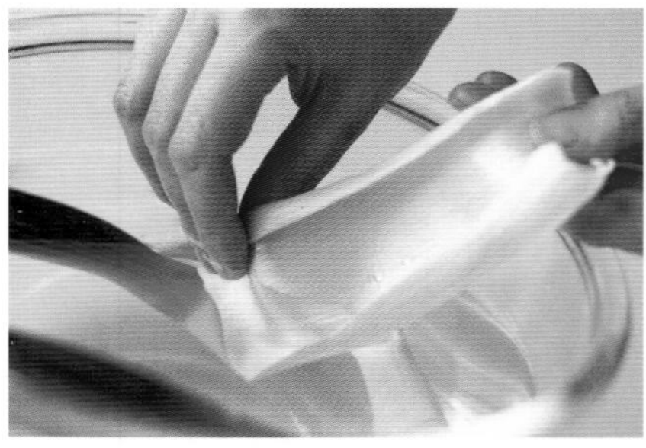

Preparing bulbs Pull off the outer leaves and wash these vegetables thoroughly before juicing, then cut into chunks the right size for your machine. It is not essential to remove the outer leaves or skin from onions, spring onions (scallions), leeks, fennel and celery, but they must be washed thoroughly as they tend to get quite dirty.

Juicing shoots Except for globe artichokes, all of these vegetables can simply be cleaned and juiced as they are. For alfalfa and cress, this will probably mean cutting the shoots from the root as the roots are likely to be embedded in soil. You will need to alternate shoot vegetables with hard vegetables, such as carrots, otherwise no juice will come out.

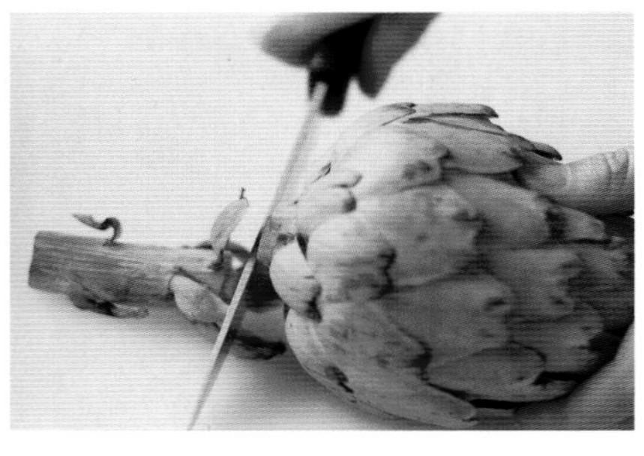

Preparing globe artichokes Remove the woody stem, then cut the rest of the flower into chunks and push through the juicer.

Beans and Mangetouts

Choose firm, crisp beans – choices include broad (fava), runner and French (green) beans. Avoid any that have been pre-trimmed or that are going soft. Buying local produce in season is the best option, because out of season beans are usually imported from countries where there might not be any regulations regarding chemical sprays. With the exception of mangetouts (snow peas), which make a fairly mild and sweet juice, beans do not taste great when juiced – you will want to mix them with other vegetables.

Therapeutic uses Traditional herbal uses of pod vegetables are as a stimulant for the nervous system, for convalescence, to treat gout and to help support the insulin-producing ability of the pancreas.

Fennel and Celery

These two vegetables make very useful juices. Their tastes are fairly strong so they are best added to other juices, such as carrot, apple or pear, at a ratio of about one-fifth fennel or celery to four-fifths other juice. Fennel tastes of aniseed, and juiced celery, when combined with other juices, does not taste nearly as strong as the raw vegetable. Buy firm, pale green produce for the best flavours.

Therapeutic uses The cleansing actions of these two vegetables are similar, and they are excellent for supporting the liver and gall bladder. Celery also has a strong diuretic action and is often used to calm the nervous system, while fennel is used to manage flatulence and nausea. When combined with carrot juice, fennel is a traditional remedy for failing eyesight. It is also used to ward off headaches and migraines, and some people believe it is helpful in alleviating menstrual and menopausal symptoms.

Onions and Leeks

All onions, including shallots, spring onions (scallions) and even red onions, produce strong tasting juices. You only need to add a tiny quantity to a general vegetable juice. Leek juice is not as strong as onion juice but has a similar taste. One of the problems

Left: Fennel produces a strong aniseed juice that can be overpowering.

with onions, as with garlic, is that they can leave a residual taste on the mesh of the machine, meaning that extra cleaning is needed. Running half a lemon through the machine can help to mop up the scent.
Therapeutic uses These bulb vegetables have renowned healing qualities. Onions are recommended for their immune-boosting qualities whenever you have a cold or the flu. They are also antibacterial and antiseptic – leeks have similar but milder actions.

Asparagus

A shoot vegetable, asparagus is available in the spring. It combines well with other vegetables but is not suitable to drink on its own.
Therapeutic uses Asparagus is used as a traditional remedy for kidney problems. The alkaloid asparagine, which is also found in potatoes and beetroot (beets), stimulates the kidneys but also turns urine a dark colour with a distinctive smell. This is not something to worry about, it is simply an indication of its successful diuretic effect.

Left: Leeks are a member of the onion family with similar healing properties.

Beansprouts, Cress and Alfalfa

You can buy beansprouts and cress in most large supermarkets, and alfalfa may be sourced in health food stores. Otherwise you can buy seeds and sprout them yourself (see right). They all give fairly strong tasting, peppery juices, so need to be mixed with other vegetable juices to tone down their flavour. They are probably easier to use in salads than in juices, but some people like to juice them for their distinctive taste.
Therapeutic uses These shoot vegetables have lots of nutritional benefits. Beansprouts are high in many minerals and vitamins, while cress is a member of the brassica family and therefore is believed to provide the same anti-cancer health benefits. Alfalfa has high levels of vitamins A, C and K, but should not be used often because it is high in a compound called canavanine, which is believed to aggravate rheumatoid arthritis.

Below: Beansprouts produce a distinctive, peppery juice.

Below: Mix asparagus juice with other vegetables for the best flavour.

SPROUT YOUR OWN

Leguminous beans, pulses, lentils and peas (not split) are not suitable for juicing, but they can be soaked and sprouted and then juiced.

1 Put one type of pulse in a large glass jar. Pour in a generous amount of cold water and leave to soak for 24 hours. Discard the water, rinse the beans under cold running water and drain in a sieve.

2 Put the damp beans back in the jar. Cover with a square of cloth, securing with a rubber band.

3 Leave the beans in a dark, warm place and repeat the rinsing and draining twice a day for 3–4 days.

4 When the beans have sprouted, put them on a windowsill for 24 hours until the shoots turn green. They are now ready for juicing.

Globe Artichoke

The globe artichoke is actually a flower related to the thistle. The heart of the globe and the soft part of the petals attached to the middle are the parts that are normally eaten, but you can juice the whole vegetable, minus any woody parts.
Therapeutic uses The globe artichoke has cleansing and diuretic actions, and is often used to help with liver complaints. It can be used as an effective pick-me-up after festive occasions or parties.

Natural flavourings and health supplements

Herbs and spices have been used for many years for flavouring food, as well as for health and healing purposes. Some of the traditional herbal remedies that have developed over the centuries are now being confirmed as active compounds, and treatments are being refined.

Culinary Herbs

They are so familiar in our everyday cuisine, it is easy to forget that culinary herbs have important health properties. Most fresh herbs go well with vegetable juices; they should be put through a juicer with hard ingredients so the machine does not become clogged up. Alternatively, they can be steeped in the juice, but don't wait too long to drink it or the value of the juice's nutrients will begin to decrease. Fresh herbs can also be finely chopped and added as a garnish. Mint and lemon balm work very well with fruit juices. Lavender flowers, borage and fresh rosemary may also be used in some fruit blends.

Above: If possible, pick fresh mint from your garden for the best flavour.

Basil Fresh basil has a pungent, peppery flavour and a sweet aroma. It is known as a soporific herb because it is very relaxing. Put it through a juicer, followed by a hard vegetable, or crush the leaves using a mortar and pestle. Alternatively, make a tisane with hot water and add this to a juice or blend.

Mint There are many varieties of this prolific herb, which is a potent digestive aid. Flavours vary but all mints have a strong, sweet aroma and cool aftertaste. Make a tisane and use it to dilute juices.

Left: Basil can either be juiced or used as a tasty garnish.

Right: Dill works well with carrot juice and aids digestion.

Parsley There are two basic varieties of parsley – curly and flat leaf, the latter having the stronger flavour. Use it sparingly. This herb is very rich in a number of nutrients including calcium and betacarotene. It can be put through a juicer, but it must be followed by a hard vegetable, such as carrot.

Chives These are a member of the onion family, and they provide a mild onion flavour. They have the same immune-supporting benefits as all types of onion and leeks.

Rosemary This herb acts as a stimulant to the nervous and circulatory systems and is also thought to relieve indigestion. As an infusion, it is traditionally used to relieve colds and headaches.

Sage Fresh sage has a pungent, slightly bitter aroma. It is an effective alleviator of sweating as a side effect of menopausal hot flushes. Make a tisane with hot water and use to dilute juices. Do not use sage if breastfeeding as it can reduce milk flow.

Dill With its distinctive yet mild caraway-like flavour, dill marries well with all green juices and carrot juice. It is a calming herb and is known to be a soporific. It also aids digestion.

Juniper berries These have antiseptic properties and can be used to treat urinary tract infections such as cystitis. Juniper berries should not be used if you are pregnant or suffer from kidney infections, as they can cause the uterus to contract.

Culinary Spices

Like herbs, spices can add wonderful flavourings to a surprising number of fruit and vegetable juice blends, and they can make an ordinary juice into something special. Many of them also have extremely important therapeutic benefits.

Horseradish This pungent root is a potent sinus clearer. Grate a little and add as required to juices but do not put horseradish through a juicer.

Chilli Ranging from fairly mild to fiery hot, it is believed that chilli spices help to build up a strong immune system and may chase off imminent colds and fevers. Use only a tiny amount in vegetable juices and do not put through a juicer or you may end up with chilli-flavoured fruit juices. Grind in a mortar using a pestle, and avoid using the seeds unless you like a very hot spicy taste.

Above: Remove the seeds from chillies before juicing, unless you are a real fan of hot and spicy blends.

Cumin Strong and nutty, yet slightly bitter, cumin is emerging as one of the most potent antioxidant-rich "super-spices" around. The active compound is curcumin. Dry-roast the seeds, then grind in a mortar using a pestle and add to drinks.

Left: Grate a little horseradish into a juice to add extra spice.

Ginger Fresh or ground ginger is pungent and quite hot. It is a warming spice that naturally lends itself to both fruit and vegetable juices, complementing citrus fruits particularly well. Use the fresh root if you can, otherwise add ground ginger or a supplement.

Above: Root ginger is hot and spicy so use small quantities.

Nutmeg Sweet and aromatic, this is a warming spice, but do not use too much as it can have very unpleasant hallucinogenic effects.

Cardamom These pods can help to relieve vomiting and indigestion. Cardamom sweetens the breath when chewed and is also used to treat colds.

GARLIC

This pungent bulb is regarded as a "super-herb" by juicing fans.

It is a potent blood thinner and immune-system supporter. It is best not to put it through the juicer as you will never get rid of the taste. Instead, pulverize it using a mortar and pestle and add just a tiny bit directly to the juice.

Star anise With a distinct aniseed flavour, star anise is useful for treating inflammation of the respiratory tract, loosening phlegm and calming peptic ulcers. It is also used to treat cramps. Grind the seeds and add to a juice.

Cloves The oil from cloves is potent and is traditionally used to numb the gums during dental treatment or to relieve the pain for young children who are teething. Its strong antibacterial properties can be harnessed by making a tisane and adding to drinks, although the flavour of cloves will dominate any other ingredients.

Cinnamon A tree bark, cinnamon helps to soothe unsettled stomachs, can be used to revive your appetite, eases digestive tract spasms and alleviates flatulence. Grind the fresh spice and add half a teaspoon to juices or blends – the flavour complements banana, pear and carrot.

Other Useful Herbs, Spices and Supplements

It is easy to add medicinal herbs to juices. Before you do so, however, make sure there are no contra-indications or interactions with any medications you are currently taking – check with your medical practitioner.

Chamomile This herb has an apple-like scent that belies its pungent, rather bitter flavour. It is a calming herb and is very safe even for children. Use a chamomile teabag, available from larger supermarkets and health food stores, or simply infuse 4–5 fresh flower-heads, then add the infusion to your juice. Chamomile should not be used by anybody who has an allergy to ragwort.

Ginkgo This is excellent for the circulation and is thought to be good for boosting memory. Simply empty a capsule into your juice and mix thoroughly.

Left: Liquorice can help to relieve allergies.

Above: Rosehips are usually made into powder or tablets.

Rosehip The reddish-orange fruit of the rose has extremely high levels of vitamin C. Rosehips are usually sold in powdered form or as tablets. Add a small amount of powder to your blend (check the packet for quantities), crumble a tablet in, or make a rosehip tisane and add it to your juice.

Ginseng A sweet liquorice-flavoured root, this is used as an energy booster, and some people even believe it is a libido enhancer. It is also reputed to help with the treatment of high blood pressure. Available in health food stores, simply empty a capsule or sprinkle some of the powder (according to instructions) into your juice.

Milk thistle This is an important liver-supporting herb which marries well with globe artichoke. It can help prevent damage to the liver from alcohol. Empty one or two capsules into your juice.

Liquorice This root has a mild steroid effect and can help relieve the symptoms of most allergies. However, it should not be used alongside steroid medication or by anyone who suffers from high blood pressure as it can cause the retention of sodium and the depletion of potassium. Liquorice is available as a root from most health food shops. Grind the root with a mortar and pestle and sprinkle a little into your drink.

Echinacea This is a classic immune-boosting herb often found as a supplement in fruit or herbal teas. It is usually taken in the winter to stave off cold and flu symptoms. Echinacea is widely available in tincture form and it is easy to add a few drops to your juice according to instructions, or you could make a tisane with hot water and add this to your drink.

A NATURAL HEALER

Grown from the wholewheat grain, wheatgrass has been recognized for centuries for its general healing qualities. It is a powerful detoxifier and cleanser and a rich source of B vitamins and vitamins A, C and E, as well as all the known minerals. Its vibrant green colour comes from chlorophyll (known as nature's healer), which works directly on the liver to eliminate harmful toxins. Once it is juiced, wheatgrass should be consumed within 15 minutes, preferably on an empty stomach. Wheatgrass juice can be powerful in its effect, and some people may feel dizzy or nauseous the first time they drink it. Sip small amounts until your body gets used to it.

Left: Kelp is a form of seaweed and is packed full of vitamins and minerals.

Other Health Ingredients

Once you realize that supplements can be added to juices, checking for contraindications first, you can become quite adventurous. It is easy to do and beats popping endless vitamin and supplement pills every day.

Brewer's yeast Very rich in B vitamins and minerals such as iron, zinc, magnesium and potassium, brewer's yeast also supplies a form of protein. It has a very strong flavour but this becomes a pleasant nutty taste when blended with fruits or vegetables.

Bee pollen This is a useful immune booster and can also help relieve the symptoms of hay fever.

Spirulina and wheatgrass One of the main superjuice ingredients, spirulina is rich in a wide variety of nutrients and vitamins. Both spirulina and wheatgrass are often used as an ingredient in supercharged, healthy juices. They are readily available in powdered form and can easily be added to juices, but you could create your own free supply by growing them at home.

Vitamin C It is extremely easy to add a little vitamin C to your daily juice, whether you use a squeeze of lemon or lime juice, a powder sprinkled into your blend or a tablet crumbled in. A non-acidic version of vitamin C, such as magnesium ascorbate, is gentler on the stomach than most others. Make sure you choose one with bioflavonoids for maximum effect.

Kelp This form of seaweed is naturally very rich in minerals, such as calcium, copper, iron, magnesium, potassium and zinc, B vitamins and betacarotene. It also contains high levels of iodine, which is vital for encouraging the normal functioning of the thyroid gland, but it should not be taken by those with an overactive thyroid. Seaweeds, such as kelp, have long been used to treat those suffering from common colds, constipation, arthritis and rheumatism.

Sambucol (elderberry extract)
During the winter when berries are not readily available or are too expensive, simply add a teaspoonful of sambucol to your juices. This is a rich source of proanthocyanins and will give your immune system a boost.

Aloe vera The fleshy succulent plant called aloe vera provides two main products: aloe vera gel, which is used externally for soothing skin irritations and sunburn, and aloe vera juice, which can be added to your juices and blends. Aloe vera juice is reputed to help relieve the symptoms of arthritis, ME and eczema, and is also renowned for soothing and rebuilding the digestive tract. Make sure you choose a certified product with a guaranteed amount of active compounds and add a dose, according to the instructions on the packet, to your drink.

FATS AND OILS

Healthy fats are good sources of essential fatty acids, which can help to clear up a range of complaints including dry skin, listless hair and low energy levels.

Lecithin This is an emulsifier derived from soya, which is ideal to add to a juice or blend before any fats. Add 5–10ml/1–2 tsp to the ingredients in a blender. It tastes pleasant and helps fat digestion.

Evening primrose oil This can be helpful in alleviating pre-menstrual problems and for allergies. Pierce a capsule with a pin and squeeze into your juice.

Walnut oil This oil has a pleasant nutty taste and is light so it does not overwhelm juices. It is a good source of both omega-3 and omega-6 fatty acids, which are useful for nervous and hormonal health. Add 5–10ml/ 1–2 tsp to a glass of juice. Store in the refrigerator.

Flax seed oil A "super-oil", this has high levels of omega-3 fatty acids. Add 5–10ml/1–2 tsp to your juice. Store in the refrigerator.

Above: Walnut oil has a nutty flavour that works well in most juices.

Juicing in a healthy diet

Following a healthy diet is one of the most fundamental ways in which you can ensure optimal energy levels, balanced moods, a zest for life and, of course, good general health. For overall wellbeing, it is also important to take sufficient exercise and to maintain a positive attitude to life.

What constitutes a healthy diet? Fresh fruit and vegetables are the most essential aspect – at least five portions a day – and drinking juices will keep you rehydrated as well as ensuring that you get the recommended amounts. These four easy-to-follow rules could help you develop a regime that will set you up for life.

1 Eat a wide variety of fresh foods to make sure you get all the vitamins and minerals you need.
2 Base your diet on fruits, vegetables, grains, legumes, nuts, seeds and eggs. If you are a meat-eater, always select lean cuts and restrict your intake of red meats. Fresh, unprocessed fish is always a healthier option.
3 Keep processed, salty, sugary or fatty foods to a minimum.
4 Drink sufficient water to stay hydrated: 1.5–2 litres/2½–4 pints/1½–2 quarts per day is the usual recommendation.

Above: Cantaloupe melons are high in betacarotene and support the immune system.

Therapeutic Juicing

In order to receive the therapeutic benefits from juices, you will need to incorporate the suggested juice on a regular basis – daily, if possible. However, remember that therapeutic juicing is not intended to take the place of eating balanced, healthy meals, but should always be an addition to your health routine.

Juices have been used by herbalists, naturopaths and nutritionists for centuries to prevent illness and alleviate ailments. However, self-diagnosis and treatment of any serious condition is not really advisable, and you should always check with your health practitioner if any symptoms persist.

Their acidity and sugar levels mean that juices can have an eroding effect on teeth. To minimize this, it is best to consume them alongside meals. You can also reduce the effect by adding calcium-rich ingredients to juices. Leafy vegetables such as cabbage, broccoli and kale are high in calcium and are also tooth-friendly. Avoid brushing your teeth for an hour after drinking a juice as the enamel on the teeth needs time to harden again.

Immune System Health and Allergies

Antioxidants found in fruits and vegetables are extremely important in supporting the immune system. There are a number of fruits and vegetables that are particularly helpful in this respect. Foods that are rich in betacarotene, such as carrots and cantaloupe melons, and dark red or blue fruits, such as cherries and blueberries, are very supportive of the immune system. Foods rich in vitamin C, such as blackcurrants and kiwi fruit, are also important. Additionally, specific compounds, such as resveratrol in grapes and lycopene in watermelons and tomatoes, are thought to help keep the immune system healthy.

The brassica family, which includes broccoli, cabbage, Brussels sprouts and cauliflower, are thought to be potent cancer fighters. Garlic, onions and leeks are all good weapons for fighting off colds, coughs and flu. If you find raw onion or garlic in juice a little too strong, try a delicious warm onion and garlic broth instead. Quinces were traditionally used to help people through periods of convalescence, and are still recommended by many people today.

Anyone with allergies, unless they are allergic to a particular fruit or vegetable, will benefit from at least five portions daily to strengthen their immune system and raise the threshold at which allergic reactions are triggered. Dark red and purple berries seem to be particularly effective in this respect.

THE POWER OF ANTIOXIDANTS

Antioxidants protect you against a number of diseases which are caused by free radicals. The plants actually make these antioxidants to protect themselves but when we eat those plants, we enjoy the benefits. Free radicals are largely a by-product of oxidization, such as when iron rusts or a cut apple turns brown. In humans this damage results in cataracts, inflammation, damage to blood vessels and cancer. Vitamins A, C and E are antioxidants but there are also thousands of phytonutrients, which are highly protective as well. Only plant foods give us these valuable nutrients and juicing is a way of ensuring that you give yourself a good level of protection.

Right: Quercitin, found in onions, is good for the lungs.

Respiratory Health

The delicate tissues of the respiratory tract can be strengthened and supported by using particular fruits and vegetables. Quercitin, which is found in apples and onions, has a strengthening effect on the lungs, and dark red and purple berries have potent lung supporting properties, which result from the high levels of proanthocyanins they contain.

Catarrh can often be reduced by avoiding dairy products, while the inclusion of garlic in juices and blends – and in your diet generally – will also help to reduce the build-up of catarrh. Turnips have expectorant properties, and radishes and horseradish, used in very small amounts, can also help to clear the sinuses.

People who suffer badly from hay fever may find that nettles are useful in helping to alleviate their symptoms.

Cleansing and Urinary Tract Health

Keeping the body cleansed of toxins is an obvious way to maintain good health. General detoxing effects can be helped along by juicing fruits that are naturally high in pectin and/or ellagic acid, such as apples, strawberries and grapes.

Liver-supporting ingredients include globe artichokes, lemons and cranberries. Fennel juice helps to detoxify the liver, and is also useful in helping to restore general wellbeing. Radishes help to support the gall bladder, which is where bile is stored before being discharged into the duodenum, where it aids the emulsification and absorption of fats.

Juices that have a diuretic action, reducing water retention and stimulating the kidneys, include celery, cucumber, cranberry, dandelion, celeriac, fennel, strawberry, peach and watermelon. In the last case, leave the seeds in for extra potassium when juicing and throw in a piece of the rind for some extra nutrients. Asparagine, found in asparagus, also stimulates the kidneys and helps to purify the blood. It makes the urine turn a dark colour, with a distinctive smell, but this is not harmful and is actually an indication that it is doing its job properly.

If you suffer from cystitis or other urinary infections, drink plenty of fresh cranberry or blueberry juice. These juices are known to help prevent bacteria from adhering to the urinary tract. Garlic is also a potent antibacterial ingredient and may be useful in treating this unpleasant and painful condition.

Digestive Health

A healthy digestive system is vital for optimal health and to ensure the maximum absorption of nutrients from foods. For both constipation and diarrhoea, add 5–10ml/1–2 tsp ground linseeds (flax seeds) or 5ml/1 tsp psyllium husks to a drink daily. Laxative effects can also be induced with plums, prunes, peaches, nectarines, figs or pears. Ginger is a traditional remedy for nausea, including morning sickness in early pregnancy.

Apples are high in pectin, malic acid and tannic acid, all of which help to normalize digestive function (and improve liver function). Fennel juice is excellent for most digestive conditions,

Above: Cranberry juice can help to relieve urinary tract infections.

Below: Apples are useful for aiding digestion and cleansing the liver.

Below: Cucumbers are full of the valuable mineral potassium.

while indigestion, impaired digestion and stomach ulcers respond well to pineapples or papayas. Cabbagin, a compound in cabbages, helps to heal the gut wall and, along with potato juice, is a useful remedy for ulcers. All fruits and vegetables are good sources of fibre, which helps to keep the bowels in good health. Making drinks in a blender or food processor rather than in a juicer will increase your fibre intake, as the fibrous, pulpy part of the fruit is preserved in the drink.

Circulation and Blood Health

A healthy blood supply will deliver oxygen, the primary nutrient, to all of your cells. For circulation and blood health, including arterial health, be sure to eat plenty of green leafy vegetables. These are rich in folic acid, which helps to lower levels of homocysteine, a substance that may be a contributor to osteoporosis. The bioflavonoids in citrus fruits, known as rutin and hesperidin, also support healthy blood vessels and so help to prevent varicose veins.

Raw beetroot (beet) and dandelion juices, along with dark green leafy vegetables, are traditionally used to combat anaemia, and if you combine these with citrus juice or tomato juice, this will serve to improve iron absorption. Potassium, which is found at fairly high levels in all fruit and vegetables, helps to lower blood pressure – watermelon, cucumber, grapes and bananas are especially good sources.

Reproductive and Sexual Health

The health of the next generation depends upon healthy parents. It is now recognized that both parents should ensure that they are in optimum health before conception. This can cause problems, because many women do not realize they are pregnant until a number of weeks after they have conceived, yet the very early stages of pregnancy are the most important for the development of a healthy baby.

For men, zinc is essential for healthy sperm and can be found in nuts and seeds. For women, folic acid is vital preconceptually and in the first trimester. It is used to help form the baby's cells, and there is now a proven link between folic acid deficiency and the incidence of neural tube defects in babies, such as spina bifida. Folic acid can be found in green leafy vegetables and in citrus fruit.

For older generations, a flagging libido may be revitalized by adding warming ginger and ginseng to juices or blends. Women with perimenopausal symptoms can try adding 50–90g/2–3½oz silken tofu or 300ml/½ pint/1¼ cups soya milk to drinks on a daily basis for their valuable phytoestrogens, as these mimic the action of the female hormone oestrogen.

Skeletal and Muscular Health

Looking after your bones is most important in your youth, when you build up maximum density, and in old age, when this density is declining. Weight-bearing exercise is extremely helpful in maintaining healthy bones.

Magnesium-rich foods are needed to help calcium utilization in bones – these include all types of green leafy vegetables, nuts and seeds. They are also good for alleviating muscular cramps, including menstrual cramps. Magnesium-rich juices or blends, taken on a daily basis, will help to improve bone health considerably.

Cucumber juice helps combat rheumatoid arthritis and other juices are also useful in this respect, including cherry, grape, pineapple and dandelion. Rheumatic pain may be eased by adding some elderberry syrup.

Dairy products and dairy alternatives can be added to juices and drinks and are an easy way to make sure you get enough calcium in your diet. Vitamin D, which is made in the skin, is vital for calcium use by bones and the best source is half an hour of sunlight exposure each day during spring and summer – although this is not always possible in some climates. If you are convalescing or susceptible to osteoporosis, add the contents of a vitamin D supplement to a juice every day.

Above: Seeds are rich in magnesium, which helps maintain healthy bones.

Above: Juice seedless black grapes when you want to unwind.

General Health

Juices help to bring a healthy glow to your skin, a sparkle to your eyes and a glossy sheen to your hair, as well as putting a spring in your step.

Fruit and vegetables that are rich in vitamin C, such as citrus fruits, strawberries, blackcurrants, green (bell) peppers and cabbage, help to build collagen for general skin health, so add these to your juices regularly. A healthy intake of vitamin C has also been proven to prevent the damage that leads to cataracts forming in the lens of the eye. To help alleviate the symptoms of eczema, try adding a tablespoon of flax seed oil to your blends each day – you can help to emulsify it into the blend by adding a teaspoon of lecithin.

Eyes need betacarotene to maintain good health, and this antioxidant can be derived in large quantities from such ingredients as blueberries and spinach. Watercress is rich in sulphur, which helps with the healthy growth of hair and nails, while cucumbers and courgettes (zucchini) are also great for healthy nails.

Grapes have long been used as a traditional rest-cure, but if you want to boost your energy levels, pears, bananas, yams and sweet potatoes are all good choices to add to your blends – try them first thing in the morning to kick-start your system. Betacarotene-rich fruit and vegetables, such as apricots, carrots, cantaloupe melons, red peppers, squashes and spinach, help to protect the skin against sun damage.

If you are on a calorie-controlled diet to aid weight loss, this can be speeded up by including filling, nutrient-rich, but low calorie juices based on fruits and vegetables. Drinking juices should help prevent you snacking throughout the day. However, if blood-sugar swings are a problem for you, dilute your juices or blends by half with water, always drink them with meals and sip slowly.

Mental and Nervous Health

A balanced frame of mind depends, in part, on a balanced diet. The saying "You are what you eat" is equally applicable to mental health as it is to physical health.

If you lack energy and are feeling lethargic, turnip and dandelion are traditional nerve tonics, while beans also stimulate the nervous system. On the other hand, if you are feeling tense, celery can have a truly restful and calming effect, while lettuce juice has a sedative action and helps to promote sleep. Oatmeal is another well-known, traditional calming remedy.

Lavender is thought to reduce headaches; try making a tisane with a few lavender spikes and adding it to a fresh juice drink. Fennel is also a traditional remedy for headaches and migraines. Nervous eczema can be a recurrent problem for some people when they're not feeling 100 per cent. This can sometimes be relieved with small quantities of potato juice. Memory and moods are helped by a good intake of B vitamins, which are found in wheatgerm, brewer's yeast, vegetable extract, molasses, peanut butter, oranges and other citrus fruits, sweet potatoes and broccoli.

Anti-stress nutrients that help to support the adrenal glands, which produce stress hormones, are magnesium, found in green leafy vegetables, nuts and seeds, B vitamins and vitamin C, found in blackcurrants, citrus fruit, strawberries, Brussels sprouts and peppers.

SYNDROME X

This is the term for a condition that could also be described as pre-diabetes, when cells become resistant to the effects of insulin. Insulin is produced by the body in response to the sugar and carbohydrates in your diet. If you tend to suffer from sugar and carbohydrate cravings, tiredness, difficulty concentrating (especially mid-afternoon), and have problems controlling your weight, then you could be suffering from difficulty in managing your blood-sugar levels. If this is the case, make sure that you dilute juices with water by half and sip them slowly instead of drinking them down in one go. Alternatively, add a dairy product or soya milk to your drink to slow down the effect on blood sugar.

Above: Celery is known to have a restful, calming effect.

Vitamins and minerals

These nutrients are needed in the diet in tiny amounts, but they are essential for health. It has been established that many people do not get their recommended daily allowances (RDAs) of many of these nutrients. Drinking fresh juices made from fruits and vegetables naturally boosts the quantity of vitamins and minerals that you take in daily.

VITAMINS

Vitamin A – Retinol

This vitamin is needed for healthy eyes, skin and mucous membranes (lungs, digestive tract and immune system). Retinol is available only from animal sources such as full cream (whole) dairy produce, oily fish, egg yolks and liver. Large amounts of vitamin A in the diet can be toxic. Betacarotene converts to vitamin A only as it is needed, and so is non-toxic.
Juicing it Betacarotene is found in orange-coloured fruit and vegetables. It is also present in dark green, leafy vegetables. As vitamin A needs fat for absorption, conversion and use, adding a little flax seed oil or similar to betacarotene-rich juices will help.

Vitamin B1 – Thiamine

This is needed to produce energy and to support the nervous system. It is mainly found in cereals and whole grains, but other non-juicing sources include legumes and meat.
Juicing it Cauliflower, pineapples, oranges, leeks, brewer's yeast and peanuts are all good sources of vitamin B_1.

Vitamin B2 – Riboflavin

Also needed for energy production, it supports the growth of healthy skin, hair and nails. It is mainly supplied by cereals and whole grains, but other non-juicing sources are fish and liver.
Juicing it Try juicing green vegetables such as broccoli, spinach and watercress and for fruits try apricots for plenty of vitamin B_2, or add small amounts of brewer's yeast to juices and blended drinks. Vitamin B_2 is also present in whole grains.

Vitamin B3 – Niacin

Niacin is needed for energy production and it helps promote a feeling of calm. Mainly found in fortified cereals, the niacin equivalent, tryptophan, is also in meat, milk and eggs.
Juicing it Juice potatoes, beansprouts, strawberries, parsley, (bell) peppers, avocados, figs and dates. Add wheatgerm to juices and drinks.

Vitamin B5 – Pantothenic Acid

Needed for energy production and to control the effects of stress, this vitamin is widely available.
Juicing it Broccoli, kale, berries, tomatoes, watermelon, celery and sweet potatoes all provide pantothenic acid, as well as wheatgerm, brewer's yeast, vegetable extract and molasses.

Vitamin B6 – Pyridoxine

Needed for processing protein, vitamin B_6 is also used for supporting the nervous and immune systems, and is necessary for healthy skin. It is found in fish, meat, poultry, eggs and whole grains.
Juicing it Oranges, brassicas, bananas, potatoes and yams provide pyridoxine. Also add watermelon and pumpkin seeds or wheatgerm to drinks.

Vitamin B12 – Cobalamine

Needed to metabolize iron and for a healthy nervous system, this vitamin is found in animal sources or yeast.
Juicing it Vegetable extract is a good source, and can be added to tomato or other vegetable juices. Dairy products such as yogurt and cottage cheese also provide vitamin B12.

Folic Acid

This is essential preconceptually and in early pregnancy for healthy foetal development. It works best when combined with vitamins B_{12} and B_6. Fortified cereals are an excellent source.
Juicing it Citrus fruits, broccoli, Brussels sprouts, lettuce, potatoes, beetroot (beets), apricots, pumpkins, peanuts and almonds are all valuable sources.

Above: Broccoli juice is packed with essential minerals and vitamins.

Vitamin C – Ascorbic Acid

This vitamin supports immunity and bone health. It is needed for skin repair and aids recuperation. It also helps in the absorption of iron, and protects against heart disease and cancer.
Juicing it Raspberries, strawberries, blackcurrants, citrus fruits, papayas and kiwi fruit are good sources of vitamin C. Also try adding beetroot (beets), tomatoes, (bell) peppers, cabbage, cauliflower, watercress and potatoes to juices and drinks.

Vitamin D

Vital in helping calcium build healthy bones and teeth, vitamin D also protects against breast and prostate cancer. It is mainly made by the skin on exposure to the sun. Half an hour per day is needed on the face, hands and arms during sunny months. The most useful dietary source is oily fish, such as mackerel and salmon, and vitamin D is also added to margarines.
Juicing it There are no food sources of vitamin D to add to juices. Vitamin drops can help to make up a shortfall, but supplements are not normally needed and excess can be toxic.

Vitamin E

This antioxidant protects against heart disease and ageing, and it also thins the blood. Whole grains are a valuable source.
Juicing it Juicing sources include dark green leafy vegetables and wheatgerm. Vitamin E is also found in all nuts and seeds and their oils (it is there to protect them from going rancid).

Vitamin K

This is essential for healthy blood clotting and wound repair, and is also needed to maintain healthy bones.
Juicing it Leafy vegetables are a good source of vitamin K, but cauliflower is the richest source. Another source is live yogurt which supports healthy gut flora, which make vitamin K.

MINERALS

Calcium

Essential for healthy bones, calcium is also important for muscle and heart health and blood clotting. Non-juicing sources include canned fish with bones (sardines and salmon) and whole grains.
Juicing it Good juicing sources include green leafy vegetables, broccoli and cabbage. Kale contains as much calcium as milk. It is also found in dairy produce (but not butter or cream) and in calcium-fortified dairy substitutes, such as soya milk or rice milk, as well as tofu.

Chromium

This mineral is used in glucose-tolerance factor, a dietary compound that is used for regulating blood sugar levels. Shellfish, mushrooms and chicken are non-juicing sources.
Juicing it Carrots, cabbage, lettuce, oranges, apples and bananas are all good sources, and chromium is also found in milk.

Iodine

This is needed for thyroid health, metabolism, energy and mental function. Non-juicing sources include fish, white rice and iodized salt.
Juicing it Vegetables contain iodine, but only if they have been grown in iodine-rich soil. Seaweed (kelp) is a good source.

Iron

Needed to make blood and deliver oxygen to cells, iron deficiency can result in lethargy and slowed mental function. Meat is the source of the most easily absorbed form of iron. Vegetarian protein substitutes, such as beans and lentils, are also important sources.
Juicing it Dark green leafy vegetables and dried fruit are good juicing sources of iron. Nuts, seeds and molasses can also provide extra iron. Uptake of iron from plant sources is doubled when it is taken with juices that contain plenty of vitamin C.

Magnesium

Needed for healthy bones, magnesium works in synergy with calcium.
Juicing it Juicing sources include green leafy vegetables, potatoes, citrus fruits and dried fruit. Nuts and seeds also contain magnesium.

Manganese

Involved in the metabolism of fats and carbohydrates, non-juicing sources are eggs and wholegrain cereals.
Juicing it Juice green leafy vegetables, peas and beetroot (beets) for manganese. Nuts are also a source of manganese.

Phosphorus

Important for bones and teeth, as well as for kidney health.
Juicing it Celery, broccoli, melons, grapes, kiwi fruit and blackcurrants are all good juicing sources of this mineral.

Potassium

This mineral is needed for healthy nerves, brain health and good kidney function. It counterbalances sodium from salt and helps to lower blood pressure.
Juicing it Juicing sources include all fruits and vegetables.

Selenium

This has antioxidant properties and is good for liver and cardiovascular health. Sources are fish, whole grains and rice.
Juicing it Green vegetables, garlic, onions, tomatoes and wheatgerm. Brazil nuts are the richest source.

Sodium

This is needed for healthy nerve function. However, we get too much of the sodium in our diet from salt, which contributes to high blood pressure and heart disease.
Juicing it Sodium is present in small quantities in all fruit and vegetables and is balanced by potassium and water. Seaweeds are alternative sources.

Sulphur

This mineral is needed to maintain healthy skin, hair and nails.
Juicing it Juicing sources are cabbage, garlic, onions, radishes, cucumbers, watercress, grapes and berries.

Zinc

Involved in all protein metabolism, zinc is very important for growth and healing, reproduction, immunity and digestion. Meat and fish are the richest sources available, but other non-juicing sources include vegetarian proteins, such as beans and pulses. Zinc is also found in brown rice and other whole grains.
Juicing it Broccoli, cauliflower, carrots, cucumbers and raspberries are the best juicing sources of zinc. You can also, try adding nuts and seeds, wheatgerm and brewer's yeast to drinks, as these are also good sources.

Below: Drinks made from grapes and berries provide sulphur for healthy skin.

super healthy juices

This chapter contains a selection of fabulous juices that have wonderful health benefits. Highly nutritious, natural additives such as wheatgrass, sprouting beans, echinacea and ginger are combined with everyday fruit and vegetables to make a range of feel-good juices for the seriously health-conscious.

Parsnip pep

Although parsnips yield a relatively small amount of juice, the juicer produces an amazingly thick, sweet and creamy drink, perfect for adding body to any raw fruit and vegetable blend. Refreshing fennel, apple and pear are the perfect foils for the intense sweetness of parsnip and together produce the most tantalizing power-pack of a fresh juice.

Makes 2 glasses

115g/4oz fennel
200g/7oz parsnips
1 apple
1 pear
a small handful of flat leaf parsley
crushed ice

Cook's tip
Parsnips are at their sweetest a few weeks after the first frost, so try a shot of this wonderful juice when you are most in need of a little winter boost.

1 Using a sharp knife, cut the fennel and parsnips into large similar-sized chunks. Quarter the apple and pear, carefully removing the core, if you like, then cut the quartered pieces in half.

2 Push half the prepared fruit and vegetables through a juicer, then follow with the parsley and the remaining fruit and vegetables.

3 Fill short glasses with ice and pour the juice over. Serve immediately.

Clean sweep

This juice is so packed with goodness, you can almost feel it cleansing and detoxing your body. As well as valuable vitamins, the carrots and grapes provide plenty of natural sweetness, which blends perfectly with the mild pepperiness of the celery and fresh scent of parsley. Drink this juice on a regular basis to give your system a thorough clean-out.

Makes 1 large or 2 small glasses

1 celery stick
300g/11oz carrots
150g/5oz green grapes
several large sprigs of parsley
celery or carrot sticks, to serve

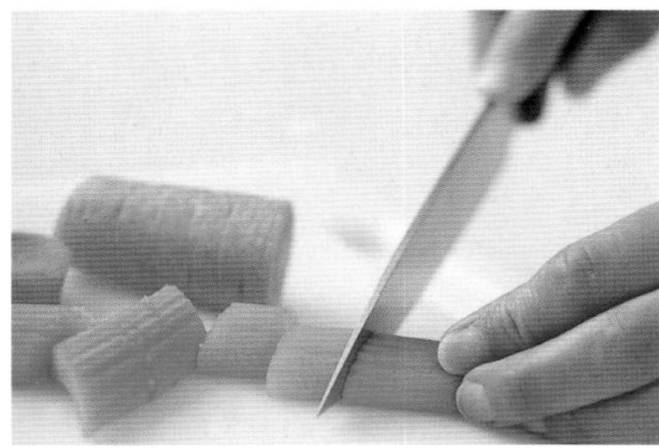

1 Using a sharp knife, roughly chop the celery and carrots. Push half of the celery, carrots and grapes through a juicer, then add the parsley sprigs. Add the remaining celery, carrots and grapes in the same way and juice until thoroughly combined.

2 Pour into one or two glasses and serve with celery or carrot stick stirrers.

Cook's tip

When juicing herbs, do not remove their individual stalks because it is the stalks that contain all the goodness and flavour – and they go through the juicing machine really easily. Parsley contains calcium, vitamins and iron and also works as a natural cleanser and breath freshener.

Bean good

Beansprouts are a highly nutritious food, bursting with vitamins B and C, and they are one of the few vegetables that actually increase in goodness after they are picked. Although mild in flavour, their juiciness works well in any nourishing blend. Mixed with broccoli, another superfood, and naturally sweet fruits, this blend is a real tonic for your skin, hair and general health.

Makes 1 large or 2 small glasses

90g/3½oz broccoli
1 large pear
90g/3½oz/scant ½ cup beansprouts
200g/7oz green grapes
ice cubes and sliced green grapes

1 Using a small, sharp knife cut the broccoli into pieces small enough to fit through a juicer funnel.

2 Quarter the pear and carefully remove the core, then roughly chop the flesh into small chunks.

3 Push all the ingredients through the juicer. Pour into glasses and serve with ice cubes and sliced green grapes.

Cook's tip

When juicing fruits and vegetables, always use the freshest ingredients you can find; that way the juice will have maximum flavour and you'll get additional health benefits. If at all possible, use organic produce. This is a bit more expensive but is definitely worth it – you can really taste the difference and your body will reap the rewards.

Wheatgrass tonic

The nutritional benefits of wheatgrass are enormous. It is grown from wheat berries and is a concentrated source of chlorophyll, which combats tiredness and fatigue, and also provides enzymes, vitamins and minerals. It has a distinctive flavour so in this juice it is blended with mild white cabbage, but it is just as tasty combined with other vegetables instead.

Makes 1 small glass

50g/2oz white cabbage
90g/3½oz wheatgrass

1 Using a small, sharp knife, roughly shred the cabbage.

2 Push through a juicer with the wheatgrass. Pour the juice into a small glass and serve immediately.

Immune zoom

Red- and orange-coloured fruits and vegetables are particularly good for protecting against or fighting off colds or flu, and are full of powerful antioxidants that are known to protect against many more serious illnesses. This refreshing, fruity drink also contains a herb called echinacea, which helps to relieve the symptoms of colds and flu.

Makes 2 glasses

1 small mango
1 eating apple
2 passion fruit
juice of 1 orange
5ml/1 tsp echinacea
mineral water (optional)
ice cubes (optional)

Cook's tip

If you are suffering from a cold or flu, or can sense its imminent arrival, echinacea can be taken in about 5ml/1 tsp servings, which can be repeated throughout the day. Check the recommended dosage on the manufacturer's packaging before use, however.

1 Halve the mango, cutting down one side of the flat stone (pit). Remove the stone and scoop the flesh from the skin. Roughly chop the flesh and place in a blender or food processor.

2 Peel, core and roughly chop the apple. Add to the blender and process together until smooth, scraping the mixture down from the side of the bowl, if necessary.

3 Halve the passion fruit and scoop the pulp into the mango and apple purée. Add the orange juice and echinacea, then blend briefly.

4 Thin with a little mineral water, if you like, pour into two glasses and serve. Otherwise, transfer the juice into a jug (pitcher) and chill in the refrigerator, then serve in large glasses with ice cubes and slices of mango to decorate.

Ginseng juice

This vibrantly coloured, deliciously tangy juice is also an excellent boost for the immune system. Ginseng is a natural cure-all that is claimed to stimulate digestion, reduce tiredness, alleviate stress, strengthen the immune system and even revive a flagging libido. Here it is added to the juice as a powder but it can also be taken as a dietary supplement in tablet form.

Makes 1 glass

1 red or orange (bell) pepper
200g/7oz pumpkin
1 large apricot
squeeze of lemon juice
5ml/1 tsp ginseng powder
ice cubes

Cook's tip

When seeding peppers, halve them, then cut around the stalk. Give the stalk a sharp pull and the core will come away easily.

1 Using a sharp knife, discard the core from the pepper and roughly chop the flesh. Slice the pumpkin in half. Scoop out the pips (seeds) with a spoon and then cut away the skin. Chop the flesh. Halve and stone (pit) the apricot.

2 Push the pumpkin, pepper and apricot pieces through a juicer. Add a squeeze of lemon juice and the ginseng powder, and stir well to mix together. Pour the juice over ice cubes in a tall glass and serve.

Red alert

This juice is perfect for those times when you're not thinking straight or you need to concentrate. Beetroot, carrots and spinach all contain folic acid, which is known to help maintain a healthy brain, while the addition of fresh orange juice will give your body a natural vitamin boost. This delicious and vibrant blend is guaranteed to set your tastebuds tingling.

Makes 1 large or 2 small glasses

200g/7oz raw beetroot (beets)
1 carrot
1 large orange
50g/2oz spinach

1 Using a sharp knife, cut the beetroot into wedges. Roughly chop the carrot, then cut away the skin from the orange and roughly slice the flesh.

2 Push the orange, beetroot and carrot pieces alternately through a juicer, then add the spinach. Pour into glasses.

Cook's tip

Only use fresh, raw, firm beetroot for juicing, rather than the cooked variety – and most definitely avoid the pickled type in jars. Beetroot juice is a stunning, vibrant red and is surprisingly sweet, especially when mixed with carrot and orange juice.

Ginger juice

Fresh root ginger is one of the best natural cures for indigestion and it helps to settle upset stomachs, whether caused by food poisoning or motion sickness. In this unusual fruity blend, it is simply mixed with fresh, juicy pineapple and sweet-tasting carrot, creating a quick and easy remedy that can be juiced up in minutes – and tastes delicious too.

Makes 1 glass

½ small pineapple
25g/1oz fresh root ginger
1 carrot
ice cubes

Cook's tip

Before preparing the pineapple, turn it upside down and leave for half an hour – this makes it juicier.

1 Using a sharp knife, cut away the skin from the pineapple, then halve and remove the core. Roughly slice the pineapple flesh. Peel and roughly chop the ginger, then chop the carrot.

2 Push the carrot, ginger and pineapple through a juicer and pour into a glass. Add ice cubes and serve immediately.

vital veggie blends

When your energy levels are flagging, these drinks are guaranteed to perk you up. Made using fresh vegetables, full of flavour and nutrients, they serve a variety of purposes from detoxing and cleansing the body to healing and energizing the mind. Ready in minutes, blends including carrot, fennel, tomato and spinach are a sure-fire way to drink yourself healthy.

Bright eyes

Thin-skinned citrus fruits like clementines can be put through the juicer without peeling, adding a zesty kick to the final mix – and saving time when you're in a hurry. This vibrant, intensely flavoured carrot and clementine combination is packed with vitamin A, which is essential for healthy vision, and vitamin C to give an extra boost to the whole system.

1 Scrub the carrots and, using a sharp knife, chop them into large chunks of a similar size. Quarter the clementines, discarding any pips (seeds).

2 Push the clementine quarters through a juicer, then repeat the procedure with the carrot chunks.

3 Pour the juice over ice cubes in tall glasses and decorate each glass with a wedge or slice of clementine, if you like.

Makes 2 glasses

- 200g/7oz carrots
- 6 clementines, plus extra wedges or slices to decorate
- ice cubes

Cook's tip

Take the tingle factor up a notch and add some extra zing by spicing up the mix a little. Peel and slice some fresh root ginger and push through the juicer with the clementines and carrots.

Smooth yet sassy, with all the colour of a brilliant golden sunrise, this mouthwatering juice will make waking up worthwhile – even on the most sluggish mornings.

Veggie boost

This simple blend makes a great juice boost. It has pure clean flavours and a chilli kick that is guaranteed to revitalize flagging energy levels. Tomatoes and carrots are rich in the valuable antioxidant betacarotene, which is reputed to fight cancer, and they contain a good supply of vitamins A, C and E, all of which are essential for good health.

Makes 2 glasses

3 tomatoes
1 fresh red or green chilli
250g/9oz carrots
juice of 1 orange
crushed ice

Cook's tip

Non-organic carrots often contain a lot of chemicals in their skins. If you use these, scrub them well or wash and peel them before use.

1 Quarter the tomatoes and roughly chop the chilli. (If you prefer a milder juice, remove the seeds and white pith from the chilli before chopping.) Scrub the carrots and chop them roughly.

2 Push the carrots through a juicer, then follow with the tomatoes and chilli. Add the orange juice and stir well to mix. Fill two tumblers with crushed ice, pour the juice over and serve.

Gazpacho juice

Inspired by the classic Spanish soup, this fabulous juice looks and tastes delicious. Fresh salad vegetables can be thrown into a blender or food processor and whizzed up in moments to create a refreshing, invigorating drink. If you are planning to invite friends for a relaxing al fresco lunch, serve this cooling juice as an appetizer; it is perfect for a hot summer's day.

Makes 4–5 glasses

½ fresh red chilli
800g/1¾lb tomatoes, skinned
½ cucumber, roughly sliced
1 red (bell) pepper, seeded and cut into chunks
1 celery stick, chopped
1 spring onion (scallion), roughly chopped
a small handful of fresh coriander (cilantro), stalks included, plus extra to decorate
juice of 1 lime
salt
ice cubes

1 Using a sharp knife, seed the chilli. Add to a blender or food processor with the tomatoes, cucumber, red pepper, celery, spring onion and coriander.

2 Blend well until smooth, scraping the vegetable mixture down from the side of the bowl, if necessary.

Cook's tip

Stir in a little extra tomato juice or mineral water if the juice is still thick after blending. A splash of red wine vinegar will intensify the flavour.

Juices made from fresh salad vegetables, packed full of valuable nutrients, are the ultimate thirst quenchers on a hot day, providing wonderfully fresh flavours and refreshing the palate instantly.

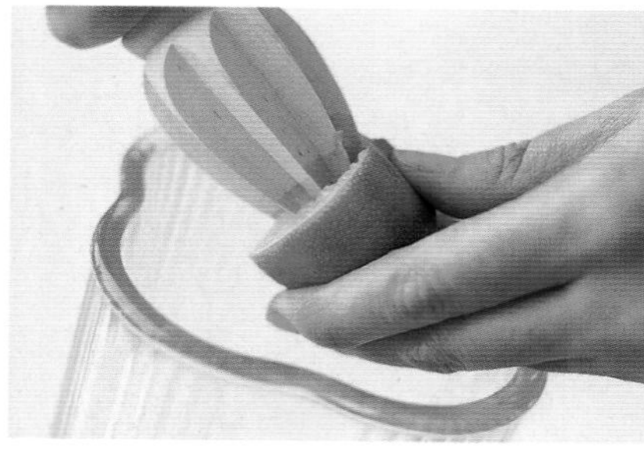

3 Add the lime juice and a little salt and blend. Pour into glasses. Add ice cubes and a few coriander leaves to serve.

Ruby roots

Beetroot has the highest sugar content of any vegetable and, not surprisingly, makes one of the most delicious, sweet juices, with a vibrant red colour and a rich yet refreshing taste. Despite its firm texture, beetroot can be juiced raw and its intense flavour combines wonderfully with tangy citrus fruits and fresh root ginger. Enjoy this juice as a natural cleanser.

Makes 1 large glass

200g/7oz raw beetroot (beets)
1cm/½in piece fresh root ginger, peeled
1 large orange
ice cubes

Cook's tip

Blood-red beetroot produces a vibrant, shockingly intense, jewel-coloured juice that is packed with vitamins and minerals, making it the perfect tonic and the ultimate health juice.

1 Trim the beetroot and cut into quarters. Push half through a juicer, followed by the ginger and remaining beetroot.

2 Squeeze the juice from the orange and mix with the beetroot juice.

3 Pour the juice over ice cubes in a glass or clear glass cup. Serve immediately.

Fennel fusion

This hefty combination of raw vegetables and apples makes a surprisingly delicious juice – fresh fennel has a distinctive aniseed flavour that blends well with both fruit and vegetables. Cabbage has natural anti-bacterial properties, while apples and fennel can help to cleanse the system. As an equally refreshing alternative, use two or three sticks of celery instead of the fennel.

Makes 1 glass

½ small red cabbage
½ fennel bulb
2 apples
15ml/1 tbsp lemon juice

Cook's tip
Buy really firm, fresh-looking fennel. If left on the supermarket shelves, it quickly discolours and turns fibrous.

1 Roughly slice the cabbage and fennel and quarter the apples. Using a juice extractor, juice the vegetables and fruit.

2 Add the lemon juice to the juice mixture and stir. Pour into a glass and serve immediately.

Apple and leaf lift-off

This delicious blend of apple, grapes, fresh leaves and lime juice is the perfect rejuvenator and is great for treating skin, liver and kidney disorders. Apples play a part in so many delicious and healthy blends that it's worth buying a large bag that will keep well in the refrigerator for several days. Most varieties can be juiced successfully so simply choose your favourite.

Makes 1 glass

1 apple
150g/5oz white grapes
small handful of fresh coriander (cilantro), stalks included
25g/1oz watercress or rocket (arugula)
15ml/1 tbsp lime juice

1 Using a sharp knife, quarter the apple, removing the core if you like. Using a juice extractor, juice the apples and grapes, followed by the coriander and the watercress or rocket.

2 Add the lime juice to the fruit and herb mixture and stir well. Pour the mixture into a tall glass and serve immediately for maximum flavour.

Mixed salad

Despite their reputation as being full of water, lettuce and cucumber contain important minerals such as calcium and zinc, alongside other crucial nutrients like vitamin K. Spinach contains plenty of betacarotene and has cancer-fighting properties. Juiced with ripe pears for maximum sweetness, a regular dose of this super juice can only enhance your health.

Makes 2–3 glasses

½ cucumber
½ iceberg, cos or romaine lettuce
2 large, ripe pears
75g/3oz fresh spinach
6–8 radishes
crushed ice
sliced radishes and cucumber, to decorate

Cook's tip

Although it can taste fairly bland in a salad, unpeeled cucumber has a surprisingly intense flavour when it is juiced. If you prefer a lighter taste, peel the cucumber with a sharp knife before juicing.

1 Using a small, sharp knife, chop the cucumber into chunks. Roughly tear the lettuce into pieces. Quarter the pears and remove the core.

2 Push all the ingredients through a juicer. Pour over crushed ice in tall glasses and serve with sliced radishes and cucumber swizzle sticks.

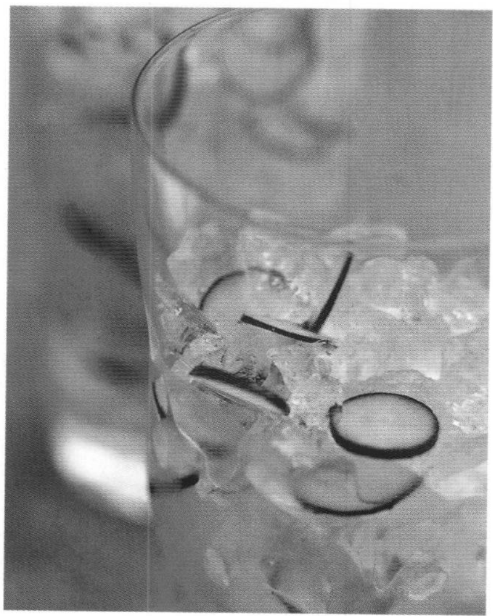

Orange blossom

Avocados are extremely good for the skin, mainly because of their high vitamin E content. Combined with parsley, asparagus and orange, this juice makes a great cleanser and skin tonic. If you have a particular skin problem, drinking this juice regularly should really make a difference – it is extremely effective and much cheaper than many skin creams on the market.

Makes 2 glasses

1 small avocado
small handful of parsley
75g/3oz tender asparagus spears
2 large oranges
squeeze of lemon juice
ice cubes
mineral water
orange wedges, to decorate

1 Halve the avocado and discard the stone (pit). Scoop the flesh into a blender or food processor. Remove any tough stalks from the parsley and add.

2 Roughly chop the asparagus and add to the avocado. Blend thoroughly until smooth, scraping the mixture down from the side of the bowl, if necessary.

3 Juice the oranges and add to the mixture with the lemon juice. Blend briefly until the mixture is very smooth. Pour the juice into two glasses until two-thirds full, then add ice cubes and mineral water. Decorate with chunky orange wedges.

Cook's tip

The orange and lemon juice in this blend means that the avocados will not discolour, so you might want to refrigerate a glass for later on. If it has thickened slightly, stir in a little extra mineral water.

Sugar snap

Sweet and juicy sugar snap peas are one of the most delicious vegetables to serve raw and they taste just as good when put through a juicer. The sweetness of the peas and the melon intensifies when they are juiced and the fresh root ginger adds a certain edge to this mellow, cooling juice. Keep the melon in the refrigerator so that it's well and truly chilled when you come to blend the juice – you won't need to add ice.

Makes 1 large glass

1cm/½in piece fresh root ginger, peeled
¼ honeydew or Galia melon
200g/7oz sugar snap peas, including pods
melon chunks and peas, to decorate

Cook's tip
Use a fresh, plump-looking piece of ginger. If it is too old, it may have started to shrivel and won't produce the necessary juice and flavour.

1 Using a sharp knife, chop the ginger. Scoop out the seeds from the melon and cut it into wedges. Cut away the skin, then chop the flesh into chunks.

2 Push the sugar snap peas through a juicer, followed by the chunks of melon and the slices of ginger. Serve chilled, with melon chunks and peas.

Celery sensation

Savoury, almost salty, celery and sweet, green grapes make an astoundingly effective twosome when combined in a blended juice. A small handful of peppery watercress adds an extra punch, but be careful not to add too much because its flavour intensifies considerably when the leaves are juiced. Celery has one of the lowest calorie contents of all vegetables, so this is a particularly useful juice for anyone on a low-calorie diet.

Makes 1 large glass

2 celery sticks
a handful of watercress
200g/7oz/1¾ cups green grapes
1 leafy celery stick, to serve
crushed ice

1 Push the celery sticks through a juicer, followed by the watercress and the green grapes.

2 Put a leafy celery stick in a large glass to act as an edible swizzle stick and half-fill with crushed ice. Pour the juice over the ice and serve.

Broccoli booster

Hailed as a cure-all superfood and a vital ingredient in a healthy diet, broccoli's strong taste does, however, need a bit of toning down when juiced. Sweet and tangy apples and lemon juice soften its flavour, making a drink that's thoroughly enjoyable.

Makes 1 large glass

125g/4¼oz broccoli florets
2 eating apples
15ml/1 tbsp lemon juice
ice cubes

1 Cut the broccoli florets into small pieces and chop the apples.

2 Push both through a juicer and stir in the lemon juice. Serve in a tall glass with plenty of ice.

Cook's tip
Don't use the tough broccoli stalks as they provide little juice and don't have as good a flavour as the delicate florets. Broccoli is packed with antiviral and antibacterial nutrients and contains almost as much calcium as milk. It is also thought to prevent some cancers, so this juice is definitely worth drinking for its health benefits as well as its wonderful flavour.

Basil blush

Some herbs just don't juice well, losing their aromatic flavour and turning muddy and dull. Basil, however, is an excellent juicer, keeping its distinctive fresh fragrance. It makes the perfect partner for mild, refreshing cucumber and the ripest, juiciest tomatoes you can find.

Makes 1–2 glasses

½ cucumber, peeled
a handful of fresh basil, plus extra to decorate
350g/12oz tomatoes
ice cubes

Cook's tip

You don't have to peel the cucumber, but the juice will have a fresher, lighter colour without peel.

1 Quarter the cucumber lengthways – do not remove the seeds. Push it through a juicer with the basil, then do the same with the tomatoes.

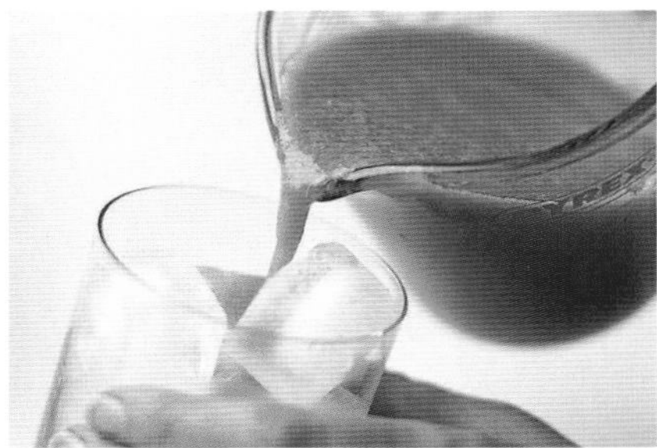

2 Pour the blended tomato, basil and cucumber juice over cubes of ice in one or two glasses and serve decorated with a few fresh sprigs of basil.

fresh and fruity

Ripe, juicy fruits make fabulous drinks, whatever the combination of ingredients but, if you're looking for guidance, this stunning assortment of recipes will set you off in a frenzy of fruity juicing. Whether using blackcurrants, bananas or exotic papayas, make sure you use the pick of the crop so your juices are both highly nutritious and tantalizingly tasty.

Fresh orange squash

Pushing oranges through a juicer rather than squeezing out the juice means you maximize the fruits' goodness and reduce the amount of wastage. Although this squash uses a significant amount of sugar in the syrup, at least you can rest assured that there are no secret colourings, flavourings and preservatives, making it a far healthier alternative to manufactured versions – perfect for children who get through gallons of squash every day.

Makes about 550ml/18fl oz/2½ cups, before diluting

90g/3½oz/½ cup caster (superfine) sugar
6 large oranges
still or sparkling mineral water, to serve

1 Put the sugar in a small, heavy pan with 100ml/3½fl oz/scant ½ cup water. Heat gently, stirring until the sugar has dissolved. Bring to the boil and boil rapidly for 3 minutes until the mixture is syrupy. Remove from the heat.

2 Cut away the skins from three of the oranges and chop the flesh into pieces small enough to fit through a juicer funnel. Chop the remaining oranges, with skins on, into similar-size pieces.

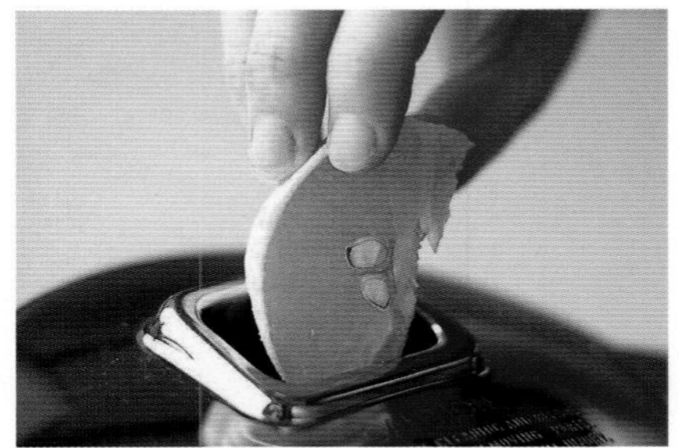

3 Push the orange pieces through the juicer, then mix with the sugar syrup. Pour into a bottle or jug (pitcher) and store in the refrigerator. To serve, dilute the orange squash to taste with still or sparkling mineral water.

Ruby red lemonade

Use blackberries or blueberries, or a mixture of the two, in this quick and easy fruit drink. A far healthier alternative to ready-made drinks, it's made in minutes and can be kept in the refrigerator for several days. If you have a glut of summer fruits, it makes sense to prepare extra and freeze it, preferably in single portions in ice-cube trays, so that children can easily pick them out, then all they need do is drop them into a glass and top up with water.

Makes about 350ml/12fl oz/1½ cups, before diluting

350g/12oz/3 cups blackberries or blueberries
130g/4½oz/scant ¾ cup golden caster (superfine) sugar
ice cubes
sparkling mineral water, to serve

1 Examine the blackberries or blueberries carefully, removing any tough stalks or leaves from the fruit, and then wash them thoroughly. Allow the fruit to dry.

2 Push handfuls of the fruit through a juicer.

3 Put the sugar in a small, heavy pan with 100ml/3½fl oz/scant ½ cup water. Heat gently until the sugar dissolves, stirring with a wooden spoon, then bring to the boil and boil for 3 minutes until syrupy. Reserve until cool.

4 Mix the fruit juice with the syrup in a jug (pitcher). For each serving pour about 50ml/2fl oz/¼ cup fruit syrup into a tumbler and add ice. Serve topped up with sparkling mineral water.

Pink and perky

This deliciously refreshing, rose-tinged blend of grapefruit and pear juice will keep you bright-eyed and bushy-tailed. It's perfect for a quick breakfast drink or as a pick-me-up later in the day when energy levels are flagging. If the grapefruit is particularly tart, serve with a little bowl of brown sugar to sweeten, or use brown sugar stirrers.

Makes 2 tall glasses

1 pink and 1 white grapefruit, halved
2 ripe pears
ice cubes

1 Take a thin slice from one grapefruit half and cut a few thin slices of pear. Roughly chop the remaining pear and push through a juicer.

2 Squeeze all the juice from the grapefruit halves. Mix the fruit juices together and serve over ice. Decorate with the grapefruit and pear slices.

Sweet, sharp shock

The taste-tingling combination of sweet red grape and tart apple is quite delicious. Grapes are full of natural sugars and, mixed with apple juice, they'll create a juice that's full of pep and zing. Grapes are also renowned for their cleansing properties, making this an ideal addition to any detox regime. For a longer, more refreshing drink, top up with sparkling mineral water.

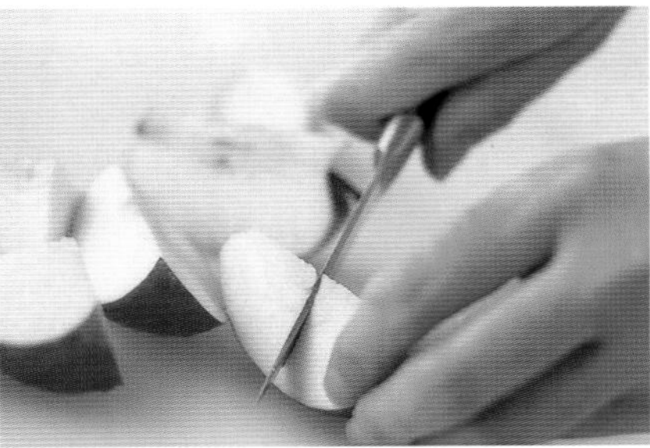

1 Slice some grapes and a sliver or two of apple for the decoration. Roughly chop the remaining apples. Push through a juicer with the grapes.

2 Pour over crushed ice, decorate with the sliced fruit and serve immediately.

Makes 1 large glass

150g/5oz/1¼ cups red grapes
1 red-skinned eating apple
1 small cooking apple
crushed ice

Cook's tip

The simplest flavour combinations are often the most delicious. Sugary grapes together with mouth-puckeringly tart apples is one of those perfect pairings that simply cannot be beaten.

Hum-zinger

This tropical cleanser contains 100 per cent fruit. It will help boost the digestive system and the kidneys, making your eyes sparkle, your hair shine and your skin glow. For the best results, use really ripe fruit, otherwise the juice may be sharp and flavourless. If the fruit is not quite ripe when you buy it, leave it at room temperature for a day or two before juicing. If you like your juices really well chilled, serve with plenty of crushed ice.

Makes 1 glass

½ pineapple, peeled
1 small mango, peeled and pitted
½ small papaya, seeded and peeled

Cook's tip
Pineapple and mango can produce a very thick juice when blended so, if using this method, you might want to thin it down with a little mineral water before serving.

1 Remove any "eyes" left in the pineapple, then cut all the fruit into rough chunks. Using a juice extractor, juice all of the fruit.

2 Alternatively, use a food processor or blender and process for 2–3 minutes until very smooth. Pour into a glass and serve immediately.

Citrus sparkle

This vibrantly coloured juice is full of the goodness of natural citrus fruits. These zesty fruits are packed with immune-boosting vitamin C, which can help to ward off winter colds and put a spring in your step, along with valuable folic acid. They are also renowned for their digestive cleansing properties. If you find this blend a little too tart, try adding a delicious sweetener, such as honey, and mix the juice well before serving.

Makes 1 glass

1 pink grapefruit
1 orange
30ml/2 tbsp lemon juice

1 Using a sharp knife, cut the grapefruit and orange in half and squeeze out the juice using a citrus juicer.

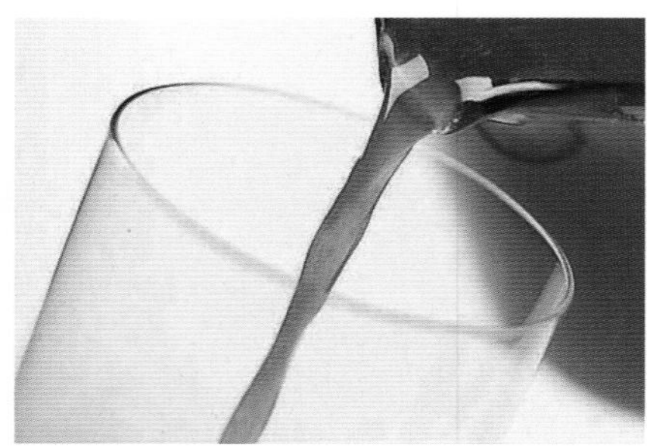

2 Pour the mixed citrus juice into a tall glass, stir in the lemon juice and serve immediately.

Opposite: Hum-zinger (left) and Citrus sparkle (right)

Apple shiner

Enjoy radiant skin and an instant energy boost with this cleansing fusion of apple, honeydew melon, red grapes and lemon. This is a good drink to make in the spring, when all of these fruits are widely available. If you cannot get hold of honeydew melon, however, you can use any other type as a substitute in this juice, as long as it's ripe.

Makes 1 glass

½ honeydew melon
1 apple
90g/3½ oz red grapes
15ml/1 tbsp lemon juice

Cook's tip
This drink is refreshingly sharp and tangy, but if you use really sweet apple and melon you might want to add a dash more lemon juice. Taste and see before serving.

1 Using a sharp knife, cut the melon into quarters, scoop out the seeds with a spoon and slice the flesh away from the skin. Quarter the apple and remove the core if you like.

2 Using a juicer, juice the fruit. Alternatively, process the fruit in a food processor or blender for 2–3 minutes until smooth. Pour the juice into a glass, stir in the lemon juice and serve.

Melon pick-me-up

This spicy blend of melon, pear and fresh root ginger will revive your body, stimulate your circulation and fire you into action. It is a great drink to serve at any time of day, whether you're relaxing with a late breakfast or reviving flagging energy levels at the end of a day's work. Serve really chilled, adding some crushed ice or ice cubes if you like.

Makes 1 glass

2 pears
½ cantaloupe melon
2.5cm/1in piece of fresh root ginger

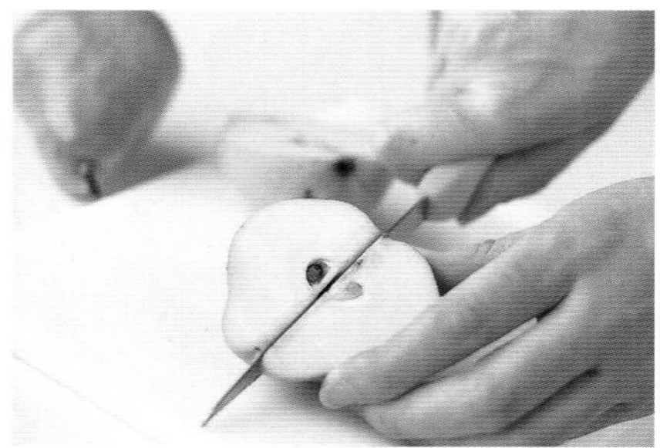

1 Using a sharp knife, quarter the pears. Slice the melon in half and scoop out the seeds with a spoon. Cut the flesh away from the skin, then quarter.

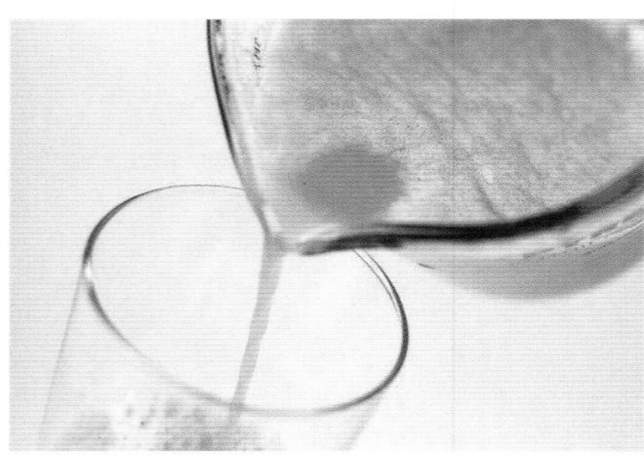

2 Using a juicer, juice all the ingredients, pour into a tall glass and serve immediately.

Opposite: Apple shiner (left) and Melon pick-me-up (right)

Blue lagoon

Blueberries are not only an excellent source of betacarotene and vitamin C, they are also rich in flavonoids, which help to cleanse the system. Mixed with other dark red fruits, such as blackberries and grapes, they make a highly nutritious and extremely delicious blend that can be stored in the refrigerator and relished throughout the day.

1 Pull the blackcurrants, if using, and grapes from their stalks.

2 Push the fruits through a juicer, saving a few for decoration. Place the ice in a medium glass and pour over the juice. Decorate with the remaining fruit and serve.

Makes 1 glass

90g/3½oz/scant 1 cup blackcurrants or blackberries
150g/5oz red grapes
130g/4½oz/generous 1 cup blueberries
ice cubes

Cook's tip

This is a really tangy wake-up drink that you might find a bit too sharp. Add a dash of sugar or honey, or top up with mineral water to dilute it slightly, if you like.

Pomegranate plus

Sometimes difficult to find, pomegranates are worth buying when you see them because their exotic and distinctive flavour is quite delicious. A reddish skin is usually a sign that the seeds inside will be vibrant and sweet. Pomegranate juice makes a delicious base for this treat of a juice, which is mildly spiced with a hint of fresh ginger.

Makes 2 glasses

2 pomegranates
4 fresh figs
15g/½oz fresh root ginger, peeled
10ml/2 tsp lime juice
ice cubes and lime wedges, to serve

Cook's tip
Pomegranates are refreshing in hot weather, especially when juiced with figs, ginger and lime juice. Serve ice-cold to quench a summer thirst.

1 Halve the pomegranates. Working over a bowl to catch the juices, pull away the skin to remove the jewel-like clusters of seeds.

2 Quarter the figs and roughly chop the ginger. Push the figs and ginger through a juicer. Push the pomegranate seeds through, reserving a few for decoration. Stir in the lime juice. Pour over ice cubes and lime wedges, then serve.

Tropical calm

This deliciously scented juice is packed with the cancer-fighting antioxidant betacarotene and can aid liver and kidney function to cleanse and purify the system. This is a quick and easy drink to make at any time of day, whether you're rushing out in the morning or relaxing later in the day. If you're really thirsty, it's a good blend to top up with plenty of chilled sparkling water.

Makes 1 glass

1 papaya
½ cantaloupe melon
90g/3½ oz white grapes

Cook's tip
Some varieties of papaya stay green when ripe, but most turn yellowy-orange and soften slightly. They bruise easily so don't buy any that have been knocked about. The seeds are edible but not particularly tasty, so they are usually discarded.

1 Using a sharp knife, halve and skin the papaya, remove the seeds and then cut the flesh into rough slices. Halve the melon, scoop out the seeds and cut into quarters. Slice the flesh away from the skin and cut into chunks.

2 Juice the fruit using a juicer, or blend in a food processor or blender for a thicker juice. Serve immediately.

Strawberry soother

Juices don't come much purer than this one. Made with fresh, ripe strawberries and a delicious peach or nectarine, depending on your preference, nothing else at all is added to this comforting blend. Rich in vitamin C, calcium and healing phytochemicals, strawberries are a good addition to any detox diet, while peaches and nectarines are great for healthy skin.

Makes 1 glass

1 peach or nectarine
225g/8oz/2 cups strawberries

1 Using a sharp knife, quarter the peach or nectarine and pull out the stone (pit). Cut the flesh into rough slices or chunks ready for juicing. Hull the strawberries.

2 Juice the fruit, using a juicer, or blend in a food processor or blender for a thicker juice. Serve immediately.

Opposite: Tropical calm (left) and Strawberry soother (right)

Minty melon cooler

The wonderfully juicy flesh of ripe melon seems somehow more fragrant and sweet when juiced. A dash of lime cuts through the sweetness perfectly and zips up the flavour, while refreshing, peppery mint makes a classic, cool companion to both. This mellow soother is equally calming and stimulating – what a combination.

Makes 3–4 glasses

1 Galia or cantaloupe melon
several large mint sprigs
juice of 2 large limes
ice cubes
extra mint sprigs and lime slices, to decorate

1 Halve and seed the melon and cut into wedges. Cut one wedge into long, thin slices and reserve for decoration.

2 Cut the skin from the remaining melon wedges and push half the melon through a juicer. Strip the mint leaves from the sprigs, push them through the juicer, then juice the remaining melon.

3 Stir in the lime juice and then pour the juice over ice cubes in glasses. Decorate with mint sprigs and lime slices. Add a slice of melon to each glass and serve.

Cherry berry trio

Strawberries and grapes have long been reputed to cleanse and purify the system, while cherries and strawberries are rich in vitamin C. This trio of plump, ripe fruits is packed with natural fruit sugars and needs absolutely no sweetening. To really spoil yourself (and undo all that cleansing power), try adding a splash of your favourite orange liqueur.

Makes 2 large glasses

200g/7oz/1¾ cups strawberries
250g/9oz/2¼ cups red grapes
150g/5oz/1¼ cups red cherries, pitted
ice cubes

Cook's tip

Each year, the cherry season passes all too swiftly, so enjoy them in their full glory in this refreshing blend of sweet, fruity, fragrant red juices.

1 Halve two or three strawberries and grapes and set aside with a few perfect cherries for decoration. Cut up any large strawberries, then push through a juicer with the remaining grapes and cherries.

2 Pour into glasses, top with the halved fruits, cherries and ice cubes, and serve immediately. To make a fun decoration, skewer a halved strawberry or grape on a cocktail stick (toothpick) and hang a cherry by its stem.

No gooseberry fool

Combine a sharp, tangy fruit like gooseberries with the sweetness of apples, greengages and kiwi fruit for a perfect blend of flavours – not too sweet, not too sharp, in fact just perfect. Even better, this drink is 100 per cent natural and is loaded with vital vitamins and minerals, meaning you can enjoy this delicious healthy tonic at any time of the day – guilt-free.

Makes 1 glass

1 kiwi fruit
2 greengages
1 eating apple
90g/3½oz/scant 1 cup gooseberries, plus extra to decorate
ice cubes

Cook's tip

Pink-tinged dessert gooseberries tend to be sweeter than the green ones, but both taste good in this refreshing drink. You might want to freeze a punnet of gooseberries so that you have a handy supply.

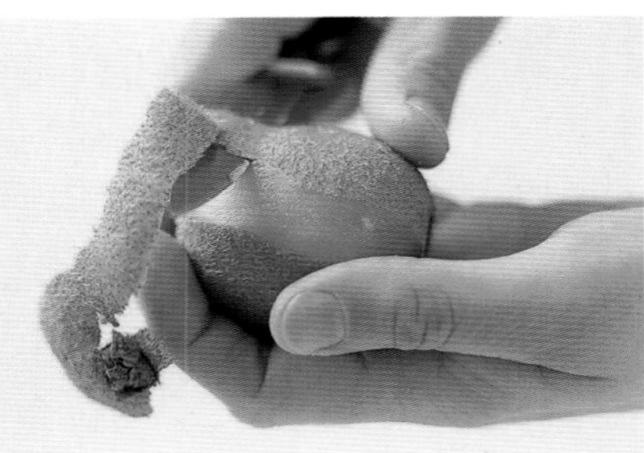

1 Peel the kiwi fruit, then halve and stone (pit) the greengages. Core and roughly chop the apple.

2 Push the kiwi fruit, greengages, apple and gooseberries through a juicer and pour over ice cubes into a glass. Add one or two gooseberries to decorate.

Golden wonder

Ripe plums make delicious juice and work really well with the banana and passion fruit in this unconventional blend. Use yellow plums if you can find them, as they are irresistibly sweet and juicy, but red ones can easily be substituted as long as they're really soft and ripe. Vitamin-rich and energizing, this drink is sure to set you up for the day.

Makes 1 large glass

2 passion fruit
2 yellow plums
1 small banana
about 15ml/1 tbsp lemon juice

Cook's tip

Passion fruit seeds might look pretty in a fruit juice, but they are not to everyone's taste. If you prefer a juice without seeds, press the pulp through a small sieve before adding to the blender.

1 Halve the passion fruit and, using a teaspoon, scoop the pulp into a blender or food processor. Using a small, sharp knife, halve and stone (pit) the plums and add to the blender or food processor.

2 Add the banana and lemon juice and blend the mixture until smooth, scraping the mixture down from the side of the bowl, if necessary. Pour into a large glass and check the sweetness. Add a little more lemon juice, if you like.

extra exotic coolers

Take juicing into another league altogether with these enticing, adventurous and utterly irresistible creations. Try delicious sun-dried tomatoes with orange and tarragon or fabulous ripe pomegranates with Asian pears. Start experimenting and you'll soon discover that the possibilities are endless.

Apple infusion

East meets West in this fabulous fusion of fresh apple and fragrant spices. Ginger is combined with apple juice and exotic, fragrant lemon grass to make a deliciously refreshing cooler. As with many of these juices, it is well worth making double the quantity and keeping a supply in the refrigerator – as you will undoubtedly be back for more.

Makes 2–3 glasses

1 lemon grass stalk
15g/½oz fresh root ginger, peeled
4 red-skinned eating apples
ice cubes
sparkling water or real lemonade
red apple slices, to decorate

Cook's tip

Bruising the lemon grass stalk releases the subtle flavour, which pervades this cooler and provides a fragrant hint of the East.

1 Bruise the lemon grass stalk by pounding it with the tip of a rolling pin. Make several lengthways cuts through the stalk to open it up, keeping it intact at the thick end. Put the bruised stem into a small glass jug (pitcher).

2 Roughly chop the root ginger and cut the apples into chunks. Push the ginger and then the apples through a juicer.

3 Pour the juice into the jug and place in the refrigerator for at least 1 hour to let the flavours infuse.

4 Half-fill two or three tall glasses with ice cubes and red apple slices, if you like, and pour in the juice until it just covers the ice. Top up with sparkling water or lemonade, if you prefer, and serve immediately.

Lavender orange lush

This fragrant, lavender-scented juice is guaranteed to perk up a jaded palate in no time at all. Its heavenly aroma and distinct yet subtle taste is quite divine. Make plenty and keep it in the refrigerator, adding a few extra lavender sprigs to intensify the flavour, if you like. Additional sprigs of lavender make fun stirrers or a pretty garnish if serving at a party.

Makes 4–6 glasses

10–12 lavender flowers, plus extra to serve
45ml/3 tbsp caster (superfine) sugar
8 large oranges
ice cubes

Cook's tip

This is an ideal drink to prepare for friends on a summer evening. Just pour into ice-cold glasses and then sit back and relax.

1 Pull the lavender flowers from their stalks and put them in a bowl with the sugar plus 120ml/4fl oz/½ cup boiling water. Stir until the sugar has dissolved, then leave to steep for 10 minutes.

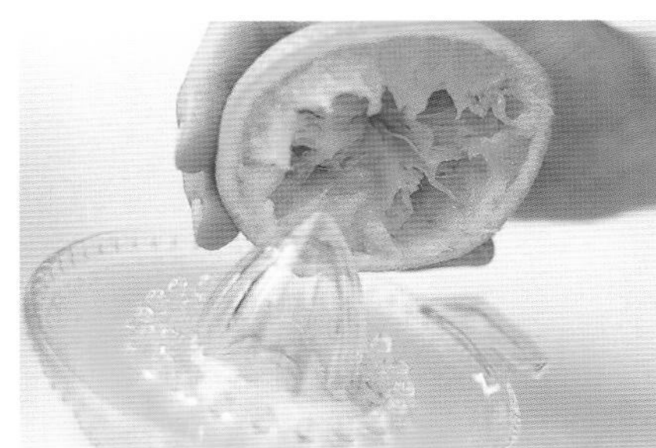

2 Squeeze the oranges using a citrus juicer and pour the juice into a jug (pitcher). Strain the lavender syrup into the juice and chill.

3 Put a few ice cubes and a couple of lavender stirrers in some glasses, top up with the juice and serve.

Peachy pleasure

When juiced together, apricots, peaches and kumquats produce the most amazingly vibrant orange-coloured juice with a flavour that has just as big a kick – and it is utterly delicious. The natural sugar content of apricots and peaches can vary enormously so you will need to add some honey to get the taste just right. Add a little at a time, then stir and, of course, keep tasting the juice until you find exactly the right flavour for you.

Makes 2 glasses

4 kumquats
6 ripe apricots, stoned (pitted)
2 peaches, stoned (pitted)
clear honey, to taste
ice cubes

Cook's tip
This drink is ideal for informal parties as well as a quick breakfast. If you are having friends round for dinner or drinks, make some funky New York cocktail-style stirrers. Simply halve some apricots, thread them on to long wooden skewers and place a skewer in each glass.

1 Using a small, sharp knife, roughly chop the kumquats and cut the apricots and peaches into large chunks. (There is no need to peel the fruit.)

2 Push the kumquat pieces through a juicer, followed by the apricot and peach chunks, alternating the fruit as you go to ensure they mix well.

3 Fill 2 large glasses with ice cubes and pour the fruit juice over the ice.

4 Stir in a little honey to the juice and taste. Add a little more honey if the juice is not sweet enough. (Be careful not to add too much honey, however, or it will overpower the other flavours and spoil the drink.) Serve immediately.

Tropicana

Even in winter this drink can brighten your day with its lively colour and deliciously tropical, fruity flavour. Any blend of tropical fruits will make a fabulous tasty juice as long as they are really ripe and ready for use. Persimmon and guavas can both be quite bitter if juiced when underripe so, if necessary, leave the fruits in the fruit bowl to ripen for a few days before using – the resulting juice will definitely be well worth the wait.

Makes 2–3 glasses

1 large papaya
1 persimmon
1 large guava
juice of 2 oranges
2 passion fruit, halved

Cook's tip
When chopping the fruit, cut some into chunky slices and reserve for decoration, if you like. Otherwise throw in some fruit chunks at the end to add some texture.

1 Halve the papaya, then scoop out and discard the black seeds. Using a small, sharp knife, cut the papaya, persimmon and guava flesh into large chunks of roughly the same size. (There's no need to peel them.)

2 Push the papaya through a juicer, followed by the persimmon and the guava. Pour the juice into a jug (pitcher), then add the orange juice and scoop in the passion fruit pulp. Whisk and chill until ready to serve.

Fragrant fruits

This blend of sweet and subtle fruits packs a surprising punch. It combines a splash of lemon and a hint of fresh root ginger to add zest and bite without overpowering the delicate, fragrant flavours of lychee, cantaloupe and pear. Other types of melon can be used in place of the cantaloupe, but you will lose the pretty colour that is part of this juice's appeal.

Makes 2 tall glasses

10 lychees
1 large pear
300g/11oz wedge cantaloupe melon, rind removed
2cm/¾in piece fresh root ginger, roughly chopped
squeeze of lemon juice
crushed ice
mint sprigs, to decorate

1 Peel and stone (pit) the lychees and, using a sharp knife, cut both the pear and the melon into large chunks.

2 Push the ginger through a juicer, followed by the lychees, pear and melon. Sharpen the flavour with a little of the lemon juice to taste.

3 Place the crushed ice and one or two mint sprigs in tall glasses and pour over the juice. Place some more mints sprigs on top to decorate, then serve the juice immediately – before the ice melts.

Cook's tip

Sweet, scented lychee and perfectly ripe cantaloupe melon shine through in this gloriously fragrant, delicately coloured blend of fresh fruits. To say that this drink is simply delicious is understating its qualities – not only is it subtle and refreshing, it is also extremely good for you. If you want to be a little wicked, however, add a dash of vodka – it will add an extra special kick.

Pink gin

Juniper berries are a vital ingredient in the making of gin and, not surprisingly, they exude distinct gin-like aromas in this fabulous drink. For a good colour, this is best made using early, forced rhubarb, which gives the juice a characteristic pink blush. Top up the gin with chilled sparkling water, or use home-made lemonade for a delicious, tangy taste.

Makes 4 glasses

600g/1lb 6oz rhubarb
finely grated rind and juice of 2 limes
75g/3oz/6 tbsp caster (superfine) sugar
15ml/1 tbsp juniper berries, lightly crushed
ice cubes
lime slices, quartered
sparkling mineral water, soda water (club soda) or home-made lemonade

1 Using a sharp knife, chop the rhubarb into 2cm/¾in lengths and place in a pan with the lime rind and juice.

2 Add the sugar, crushed juniper berries and 90ml/6 tbsp water. Cover with a tightly fitting lid and cook for 6–8 minutes until the rhubarb is just tender. (Test by prodding the rhubarb with the tip of a knife.)

3 Transfer the rhubarb to a food processor or blender and process to form a smooth purée. Press the mixture through a coarse sieve into a bowl and set the strained juice aside until completely cooled.

4 Half-fill medium glasses with the juice. Add ice cubes and lime slices and top up with sparkling mineral water, soda water or lemonade. Serve immediately.

Cook's tip

If the rhubarb syrup is stored for a couple of days in the refrigerator after straining, the juniper flavour will become more pronounced. The overall intensity is better if the drink is made with just rhubarb, but you could use a mixture of apple and rhubarb, if you prefer.

Passion fruit and orange crush

The scent and taste of this juice achieves that perfect balance of aromas and flavours. Sweet, zesty orange juice sits in perfect harmony with aromatic cardamom and intensely fragrant passion fruit to make the most heavenly juice imaginable. And, as well as the fabulous flavour and glorious colour, you get a generous shot of valuable vitamin C.

Makes 2 glasses

15ml/1 tbsp cardamom pods
15ml/1 tbsp caster (superfine) sugar
2 passion fruit
4 large oranges
ice cubes
halved orange slices, to decorate

1 Crush the cardamom pods in a mortar with a pestle or place them in a small, metal bowl and pound with the end of a rolling pin until the seeds are exposed.

2 Put the cardamom pods, with any stray seeds, in a small pan. Add the sugar and stir in 90ml/6 tbsp water. Cover and simmer for 5 minutes.

Cook's tip

The dark seeds in passion fruit look pretty when suspended in the juice and are perfectly edible, but they do not offer any nutrition and can get stuck between your teeth. If you don't want them in the drink, press the pulp through a small sieve with the back of a wooden spoon and just use the juice.

Sweet yet sharp, delicate yet robust, mouth-puckering yet refreshing – each and every sip of this unbelievably delicious blend will delight you.

3 Halve the passion fruit and scoop the pulp into a small jug (pitcher). Squeeze the oranges in a citrus juicer or by hand and tip the juice into the jug. Strain the cardamom syrup through a fine sieve into the fruit juice and whisk the mixture to distribute the passion fruit and make a light froth.

4 Half-fill tall glasses with ice cubes and pour over the juice. Slip the orange slices into the glasses to serve as edible decoration.

Honey and watermelon tonic

This refreshing juice will help to cool the body, calm the digestion and cleanse the system – and may even have aphrodisiac qualities. What more could you ask from a juice? It even looks enticing. The real magic of this drink, however, lies in its flavour. The light, watermelon taste is fresh on the palate, while the sticky, warm honey warms the throat – but it is the tart lime that gives it that edge.

Makes 4 glasses

1 watermelon
1 litre/1¾ pints/4 cups chilled water
juice of 2 limes
clear honey
ice cubes, to serve

1 Using a sharp knife, chop the watermelon into chunks, cutting off the skin and discarding the black seeds.

2 Place the watermelon chunks in a large bowl, pour the chilled water over and leave to stand for 10 minutes.

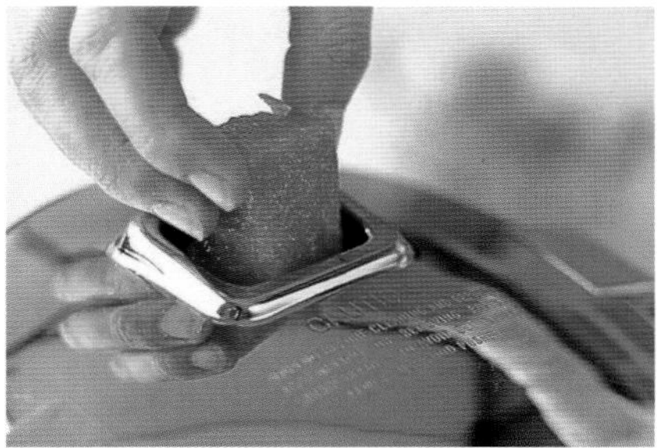

3 Strain the watermelon chunks, then push them through a juicer.

4 Stir in the lime juice and sweeten to taste with honey. Pour into a jug (pitcher), add ice cubes and stir. Serve in wide, chunky glasses.

Cook's tip

If the weather is really hot, why not serve this as a frozen slush? Freeze, stirring often, and when crystals begin to form serve immediately.

Watermelon and star anise fizz

The delicate taste of watermelon becomes surprisingly intense when juiced, so to balance it, additional flavours need to be equally pronounced. A light syrup infused with scented star anise is the perfect choice. For maximum impact, make sure the star anise is really fresh as its liquorice-like flavour and aroma tend to fade with age.

Makes 2 tall glasses

15g/½oz star anise
15ml/1 tbsp caster (superfine) sugar
500g/1¼lb wedge of watermelon
sparkling mineral water

Cook's tip

Sweet, scented, frothy pink bubbles make this heavenly juice perfect as a non-alcoholic cocktail to serve at parties. Or enjoy it as a cooling thirst-quencher on a long, hot summer afternoon.

1 Roughly crush the star anise in a mortar using a pestle, or place it in a small metal bowl and pound with the end of a rolling pin.

2 Put the crushed spice in a small pan and add the sugar and 90ml/6 tbsp water. Bring to the boil, stirring, then let it bubble for about 2 minutes. Remove the pan from the heat and leave to steep for 10 minutes.

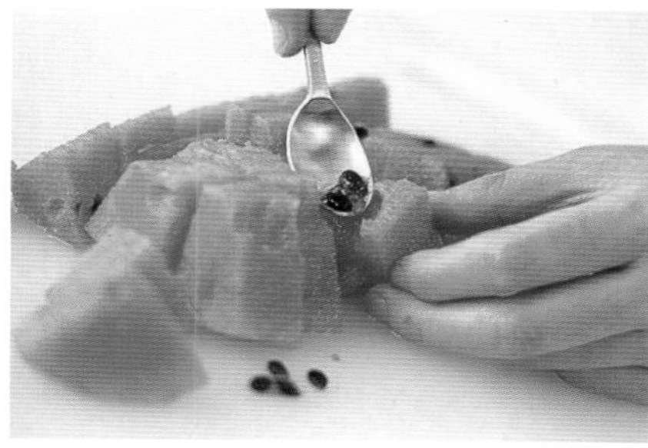

3 Cut off and discard the rind from the watermelon and, using a small, sharp knife, cut the flesh into chunks of roughly the same size, removing all of the hard black seeds.

4 Push the melon chunks through a juicer. Strain the anise syrup through a fine sieve and pour it into the melon juice. Stir well to mix the flavours together thoroughly.

5 Fill two glasses two-thirds full with the juice, then top up with sparkling water and serve immediately.

Kiwi and stem ginger spritzer

The delicate, refreshingly tangy flavour of kiwi fruit becomes sweeter and more intense when the flesh is juiced. Choose plump, unwrinkled fruits that give a little when gently pressed as under-ripe fruits will produce a slightly bitter taste. A single kiwi fruit contains more than one day's vitamin C requirement, so this juice will really boost the system.

Makes 1 tall glass

2 kiwi fruit
1 piece preserved stem ginger, plus 15ml/
  1 tbsp syrup from the ginger jar
sparkling mineral water

1 Using a sharp knife, roughly chop the kiwi fruit and the ginger. (For a better colour you can peel the kiwi fruit first, but this is not essential.)

2 Push the ginger and kiwi fruit through a juicer and pour the juice into a jug (pitcher). Stir in the ginger syrup.

3 Pour the juice into a tall glass, then top up with sparkling mineral water and serve immediately.

Cook's tip

Kiwis are a subtropical fruit, not a tropical one, so it is best to store them in the refrigerator before using. If you want them to ripen quickly, store in a paper bag with a ripe apple, pear or banana.

Spiced pomegranate and Asian pear fizz

Sweet but with a milder flavour than European pears, Asian pears make a good partner for the fresh tang of pomegranates. Juice the fruits in advance if you have the time, so the spice can mellow into the fruits, all ready for topping up with fizzy tonic water.

Makes 2 glasses

2 Asian pears
1.5ml/¼ tsp ground allspice
1 pomegranate
5–10ml/1–2 tsp clear honey
ice cubes
tonic water
pear wedges and pomegranate seeds, to decorate

Cook's tip
Pears provide significant amounts of vitamin C and potassium, and combine well with most other imgredients as long as the flavours are not too overpowering.

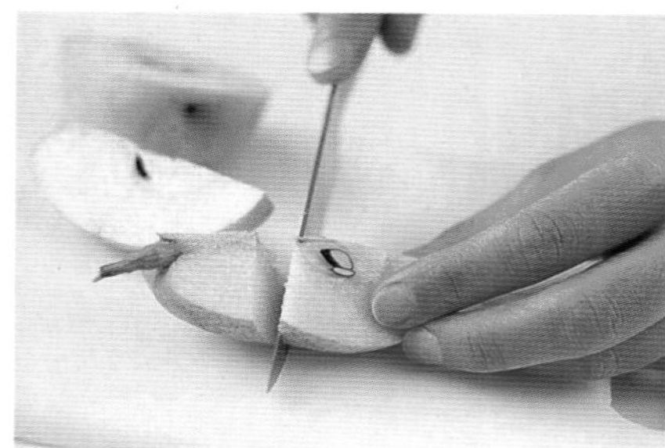

1 Using a small, sharp knife, chop the pears into large chunks. Mix the allspice in a jug (pitcher) with 15ml/1 tbsp boiling water.

2 Halve the pomegranate. Working over the jug to catch the juices, peel away the skin and layers of pith to leave the clusters of seeds.

3 Push the pears and pomegranate seeds through a juicer and mix together in the jug with the allspice. Stir in a little honey to sweeten, then chill.

4 Pour the juice into glasses until two-thirds full. Serve with ice cubes, pear wedges and pomegranate seeds to decorate. Top up with tonic water.

Elderflower, plum and ginger juice

Captured in cordials and juices, the aromatic flavour of elderflowers can be enjoyed all year round. Here it is used with fresh root ginger to give an exotic boost to sweet, juicy plums. Serve this juice just as it is over plenty of crushed ice or top up with sparkling water, if you prefer a more diluted drink. It is an utterly delicious and wonderfully uplifting blend.

Makes 2–3 glasses

15g/½oz fresh root ginger
500g/1lb 2oz ripe plums
125ml/4½fl oz/generous ½ cup sweetened elderflower cordial
ice cubes
sparkling water or tonic water
mint sprigs and plum slices, to decorate

Cook's tip
The elder is a tree or bush with perfumed, yellowish-white flowers and tiny black-violet berries, both of which are thought to be medicinal.

1 Roughly chop the ginger without peeling. Halve and stone (pit) the plums.

2 Push half the plums through a juicer, followed by the ginger then the remaining plums. Mix the juice with the elderflower cordial in a jug (pitcher).

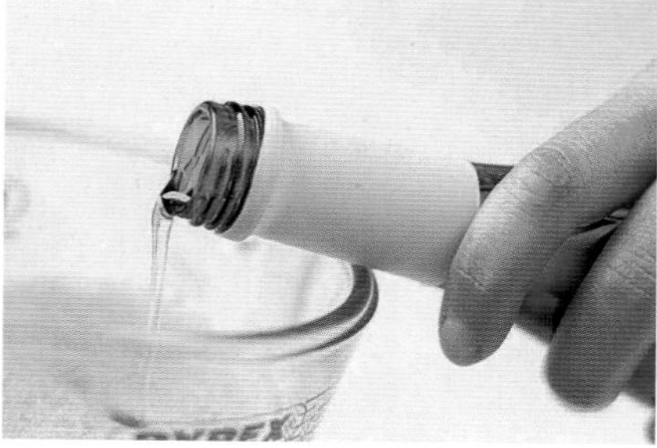

3 Place the ice cubes into two large or three medium-sized glasses. Pour over the juice until the glasses are two-thirds full. Place the mint sprigs and plum slices on top to decorate and top up with sparkling mineral water or tonic water. Serve immediately.

Red hot chilli pepper

Sweet red peppers make a colourful, light juice that's best mixed with other ingredients for a full flavour impact. Courgettes add a subtle, almost unnoticeable body to the drink, while chilli and radishes add a wonderful kick of peppery heat. Freshly squeezed orange juice gives a delicious underlying zest to this extremely drinkable beverage.

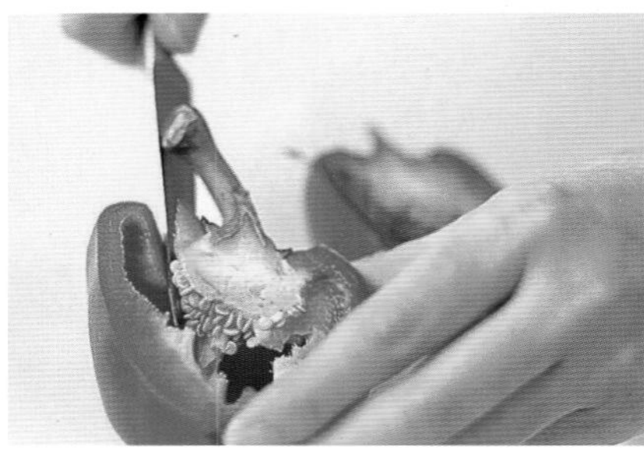

1 Halve the red peppers, remove the cores and seeds, quarter the pieces and push them through a juicer with the chilli. Cut the courgettes into chunks, halve the radishes and push them through the juicer.

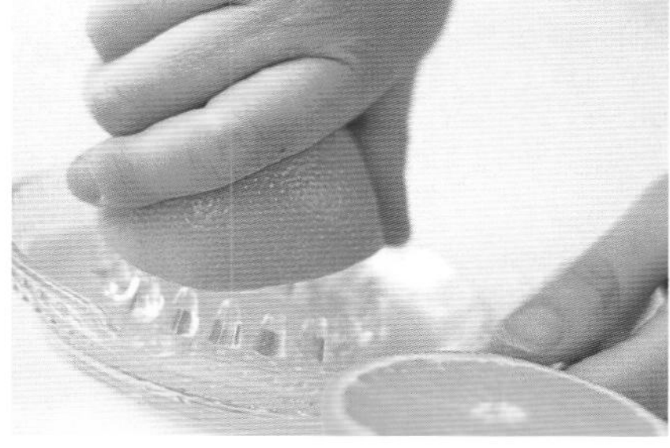

2 Squeeze the orange and stir the juice into the vegetable juice. Fill two or three glasses with ice, pour over the juice and serve immediately.

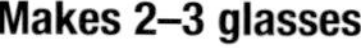

Makes 2–3 glasses

2 red (bell) peppers
1 fresh red chilli, seeded
150g/5oz courgettes (zucchini)
75g/3oz radishes
1 orange
ice cubes

Cook's tip

When working with chillies, always wash your hands thoroughly after chopping them. Avoid touching your eyes or any other delicate area because it really will sting.

Tarragon, orange and sun-dried tomato juice

Lovers of tomato juice are sure to get hooked on this flavour-packed, vitalizing blend. Fresh orange makes it irresistibly moreish and adds extra vitamin C, while tarragon adds a lovely aromatic note. Add a dash of Tabasco or chilli sauce instead of the ground black pepper if you simply cannot resist the classic combination of chilli and tomato.

Makes 2 glasses

4 large sprigs of tarragon, plus extra to garnish
500g/1lb 2oz tomatoes
2 large oranges
15ml/1 tbsp sun-dried tomato paste
ice cubes
ground black pepper

1 Pull the tarragon leaves from their stalks. Roughly chop the tomatoes. Push them through a juicer, alternating with the tarragon leaves.

2 Squeeze the juice from the oranges by hand or using a citrus juicer. Stir into the tomato and tarragon juice. Add the sun-dried tomato paste and stir well to mix all the ingredients together.

3 Place ice cubes into two glasses and pour over the juice. Serve immediately with pretty stirrers (if you have them), a sprinkling of black pepper to taste and tarragon sprigs to garnish.

perfect party drinks

If you're entertaining a large crowd, whizzing up a choice of interesting party brews is a sure-fire way to get the occasion off to a lively start. From long and refreshing spritzers to short, punchy tipples, this chapter offers a feast of innovative choices that include a couple of fresh fruit juices for partygoers who prefer not to drink alcohol.

Lemon vodka

Very similar to the deliciously moreish Italian liqueur, Limoncello, this lemon vodka should be drunk in small quantities due to its hefty alcoholic punch. Blend the sugar, lemons and vodka and keep in a bottle in the refrigerator, ready for pouring over crushed ice or topping up with soda or sparkling water. It is also delicious drizzled over melting vanilla ice cream.

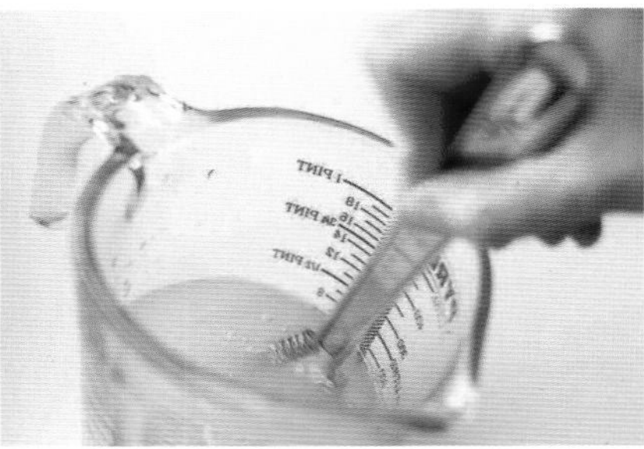

1 Squeeze the lemons using a citrus juicer. Pour the juice into a jug (pitcher), add the sugar and whisk well until all the sugar has dissolved.

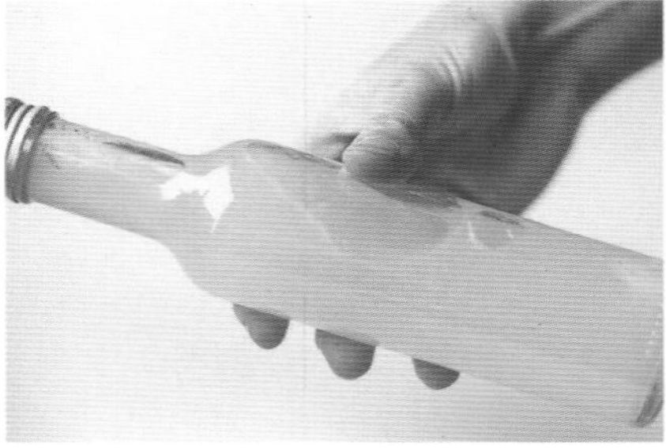

2 Strain the sweetened lemon juice into a clean bottle or narrow-necked jar and add the vodka. Shake the mixture well to combine, and chill for up to 2 weeks.

3 To serve, fill small glasses with ice and pour the lemon vodka over.

Makes 12–15 small glasses

10 large lemons
275g/10oz/generous 1¼ cups caster (superfine) sugar
250ml/8fl oz/1 cup vodka
ice cubes

Cook's tip

Pure, clear vodka and zesty lemon juice make a tantalizing spirit that tastes like bottled sunshine. If you like, bruise a couple of mint leaves and add to the glass before pouring the vodka – this will add a delicious freshness to the drink.

Apple-tice

Even the dullest of eating apples seem to juice well. With the addition of a fresh mint syrup and sparkling cider, any apple juice can be transformed into a distinctly exciting, mildly alcoholic blend that makes an excellent party drink. The recipe allows you to choose how much cider you add to each glass, which makes it easier to control your alcohol consumption.

Makes 6–8 glasses

25g/1oz/1 cup mint leaves, plus extra mint sprigs, to decorate
15g/½oz/1 tbsp caster (superfine) sugar
6 eating apples
ice cubes
1 litre/1¾ pints/4 cups dry (hard) cider

1 Using a pair of kitchen scissors, roughly snip the mint into a heatproof jug (pitcher). Add the sugar to the jug, then pour over 200ml/7fl oz/scant 1 cup of boiling water. Stir well until the sugar has dissolved, then leave to stand until cool.

2 Drain the mint from the syrup and discard the mint leaves. Using a small, sharp knife, core the apples, chop them into chunks of roughly the same size and push them through a juicer.

3 Mix the apple juice and mint-flavoured syrup in a large jug and chill (preferably overnight, but for at least 1–2 hours) until ready to serve.

4 To serve, add ice cubes and mint sprigs and top up with cider.

Cook's tip

If you'd prefer a non-alcoholic version of this drink, top up the glasses with sparkling mineral water, ginger ale or lemonade instead of cider.

Cranberry and apple spritzer

Don't forget to look after the non-drinkers at your party – all too often they're left with just the mixers, fizzy drinks or tap water. This colourful, zingy cooler combines tangy cranberries with fresh juicy apples and a subtle, fragrant hint of vanilla. Topped up with sparkling mineral water, this is one spritzer that's sure to keep everyone happy.

Makes 6–8 glasses

6 red eating apples
375g/13oz/3½ cups fresh or frozen cranberries, plus extra to decorate
45ml/3 tbsp vanilla syrup
ice cubes
sparkling mineral water

Cook's tip

To make vanilla syrup, heat a vanilla pod (bean) with sugar and water in a pan until the sugar dissolves. Simmer for 5 minutes then leave to cool.

1 Quarter and core the apples then cut the flesh into pieces small enough to fit through a juicer. Push the cranberries and apple chunks through the juicer. Add the vanilla syrup to the juice and chill until ready to serve.

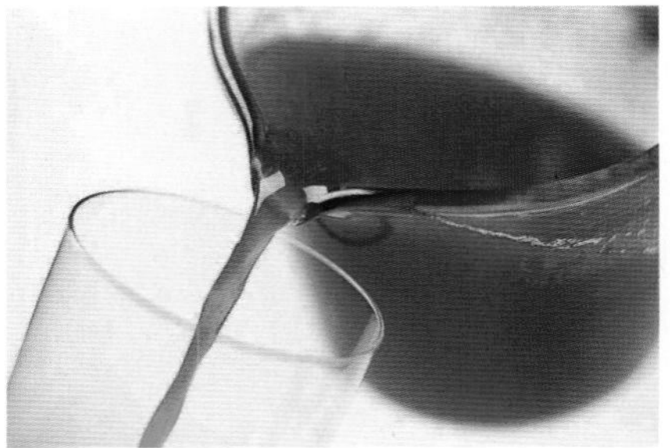

2 Pour the juice into glasses and add one or two ice cubes to each. Top up with sparkling mineral water and decorate with extra cranberries, threaded on to cocktail sticks (toothpicks). Serve immediately.

Pink perfection

Make plenty of freshly juiced blends like this gorgeous combination and your guests will keep coming back for more. Raspberry and grapefruit juice make a great partnership, particularly if you add a little cinnamon syrup to counteract any tartness in the fruit.

Makes 8 tall glasses

1 cinnamon stick
50g/2oz/¼ cup caster (superfine) sugar
4 pink grapefruits
250g/9oz/1½ cups fresh or frozen raspberries
wedge of watermelon
crushed ice
borage flowers, to decorate (optional)

Cook's tip

Make non-alcoholic drinks more interesting by dressing them up with extra fruits and decorations. As an alternative to watermelon, serve other stirrers such as cinnamon sticks, or provide stirrers made from sugar so guests can sweeten their drinks to suit their own personal preference.

1 Put the cinnamon stick in a small pan with the sugar and 200ml/7fl oz/scant 1 cup water. Heat gently until the sugar has dissolved, then bring to the boil and boil for 1 minute. Reserve to cool.

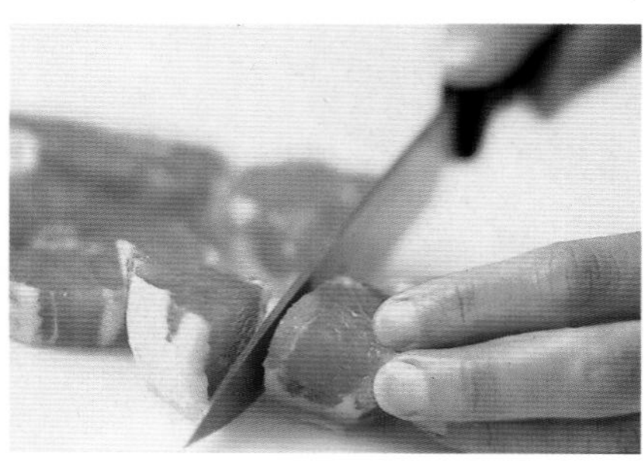

2 Cut away the skins from the pink grapefruits. Cut the flesh into pieces small enough to fit through a juicer funnel. Juice the grapefruits and raspberries and pour into a small glass jug (pitcher).

3 Remove the cinnamon from the syrup and add the syrup to the grapefruit and raspberry juice in the jug.

4 Carefully slice the watermelon into long thin wedges and place in eight tall glasses. Half-fill the glasses with the crushed ice and sprinkle with borage flowers, if you like. Pour over the pink fruit juice and serve immediately with plenty of napkins to allow your guests to eat the watermelon wedges.

Peach bellini

Serve this classic, fabulous cocktail when peaches are at their most delicious and best. Preserved stem ginger and peach juice ice cubes make an unusual twist, so allow plenty of time for them to freeze before serving. If using both brandy and sparkling wine is a little too alcoholic for your taste, top up the cocktail with sparkling mineral water instead of the wine, or alternatively omit the brandy. In fact, any combination would be equally delicious.

Makes 8–10 glasses

75g/3oz preserved stem ginger (about 5 pieces), sliced
6 large ripe peaches
150ml/¼ pint/⅔ cup peach brandy or regular brandy
1 bottle sparkling wine

Cook's tip
When the ice cubes start to melt you will get an extra hit of peach and ginger juice in your drink. Drink this cocktail slowly to allow all of the flavours to merge.

1 Place one or two slices of ginger in all the sections of an ice-cube tray. Halve and stone (pit) the peaches then push through a juicer. Make 200ml/7fl oz/ scant 1 cup of the peach juice up to 300ml/½ pint/1¼ cups with water. Pour into the ice-cube tray. Freeze.

2 When frozen solid, carefully remove the ice cubes from the tray and divide among eight to ten wine glasses. Stir the brandy into the remaining peach juice, mix well and pour over the ice cubes. Top up with the sparkling wine and serve immediately.

Tropical storm

Whisky and ginger makes a popular flavour combination in party drinks and cocktails, either served neat or blended with other ingredients to dilute the intense flavour. This incredibly refreshing creation with mango and lime has, not surprisingly, plenty of kick.

Makes 8 tall glasses

2 large ripe mangoes
2 papayas
2 limes
150ml/¼ pint/⅔ cup ginger wine
105ml/7 tbsp whisky or Drambuie
ice cubes
lime slices and mango and papaya wedges, to decorate
soda water (club soda)

Cook's tip
Mango and papaya sometimes collects inside the juicer rather than flowing easily into the container. If this happens, pour a little cold water through the juicer funnel.

1 Halve the mangoes either side of the flat stone (pit). Using a spoon, scoop out the flesh from the halves and cut from around the stone using a small, sharp knife. Chop roughly.

2 Halve the papaya and discard the pips (seeds). Remove the skin and roughly chop the flesh. Cut away the skins from the limes and halve.

3 Push the mangoes, papayas and limes through a juicer. Pour into a jug (pitcher), add the ginger wine and whisky or Drambuie and chill until ready to serve.

4 Place plenty of ice cubes and long wedges of mango and papaya and slices of lime into tall glasses. Pour over the juice until the glasses are two-thirds full. Top up with soda water and serve.

Happy days

Set a midsummer drinks party off to a good start with this fabulously fruity blend. It's packed with summer fruits and flavoured with refreshingly light, but highly intoxicating, Limoncello – a welcome alternative to the more traditional spirits used in party blends.

Makes 8 glasses

250g/9oz/generous 2 cups redcurrants
675g/1½lb/6 cups strawberries
200ml/7fl oz/scant 1 cup Limoncello liqueur
ice cubes
small handful of mint or lemon balm
I litre/1¾ pints/4 cups lemonade or cream soda

1 Using a fork, strip the redcurrants from their stalks. Reserve 50g/2oz/½ cup. Hull the strawberries and reserve 200g/7oz/1¾ cups. Push the remainder through a juicer with the redcurrants. Pour into a glass punch bowl or jug (pitcher) and stir in the liqueur. Chill until ready to serve.

2 Halve the reserved strawberries and add to the juice with the redcurrants, plenty of ice cubes and the mint or lemon balm. Top up with lemonade or cream soda, and serve.

Cook's tip

Limoncello is an intensely tangy, very alcoholic Italian lemon liqueur. It's great served on its own over plenty of crushed ice or, more unusually, in this fruity punch. If you can't find it, use a well-flavoured orange liqueur such as Cointreau or Grand Marnier instead.

Grand Marnier, papaya and passion fruit punch

The term "punch" comes from the Hindi word *panch* (five), relating to the five ingredients traditionally contained in the drink – alcohol, lemon or lime, tea, sugar and water. The ingredients may have altered somewhat over the years but the best punches still combine a mixture of spirits, flavourings and an innocent top-up of fizz or juice.

Makes about 15 glasses

2 large papayas
4 passion fruit
300g/11oz lychees, peeled and pitted
300ml/½ pint/1¼ cups freshly squeezed orange juice
200ml/7fl oz/scant 1 cup Grand Marnier or other orange-flavoured liqueur
8 whole star anise
2 small oranges
ice cubes
1.5 litres/2½ pints/6¼ cups soda water (club soda)

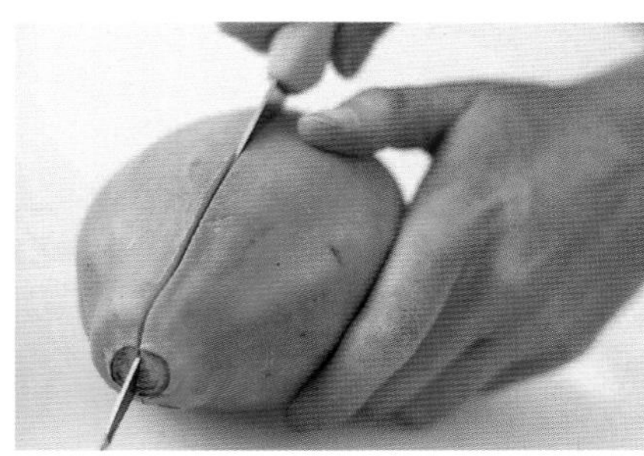

1 Halve the papayas and discard the seeds. Halve the passion fruit and press the pulp through a sieve into a small punch bowl or a pretty serving bowl.

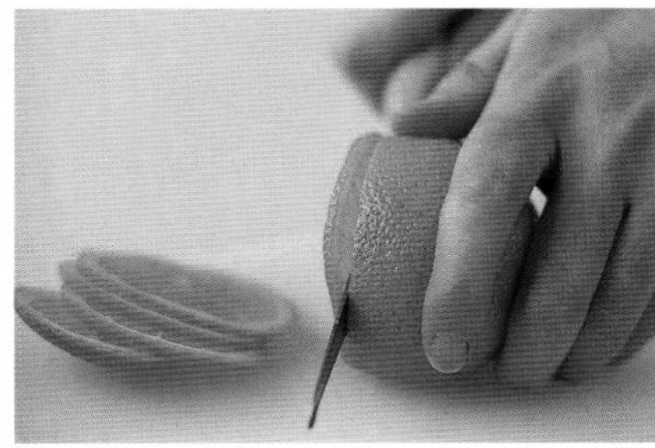

2 Push the papayas through a juicer, adding 100ml/7 tbsp water to help the pulp through. Juice the lychees. Add the juices to the bowl with the orange juice, liqueur and star anise. Thinly slice the oranges and add to the bowl. Chill for at least 1 hour or until ready to serve.

3 Add plenty of ice cubes to the bowl and top up with soda water. Ladle into punch cups or small glasses to serve.

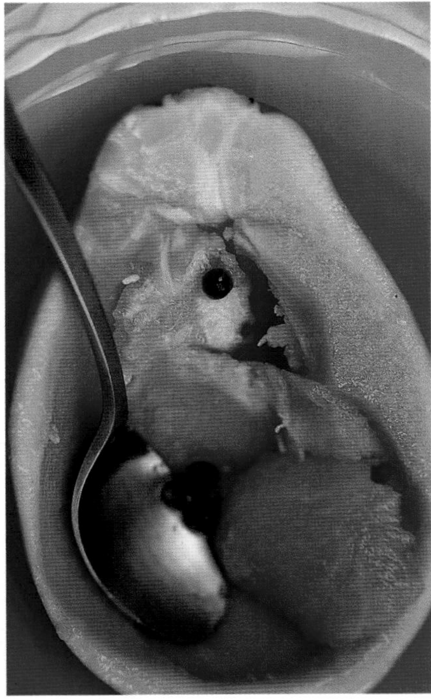

Apple-spiced beer

Lager takes on a whole new dimension in this fun and fruity cooler. Diluted with freshly made apple juice and flavoured with ginger and star anise, it's a great drink for anyone who wants to pace themselves through a party. The spiced apple juice can be made several hours in advance and chilled in a serving jug, ready for topping up at the last minute.

Makes 8–10 tall glasses

8 eating apples
25g/1oz fresh root ginger
6 whole star anise
800ml/1⅓ pints/3½ cups lager
crushed ice

1 Quarter and core the apples and, using a small, sharp knife, cut the flesh into pieces small enough to fit through a juicer. Roughly chop the ginger. Push half the apples through the juicer, then juice the ginger and the remaining apples.

2 Put 105ml/7 tbsp of the juice in a small pan with the star anise and heat gently until almost boiling. Add to the remaining juice in a large jug (pitcher) and chill for at least 1 hour.

3 Add the lager to the juice and stir gently to help disperse the froth. Pour over crushed ice in tall glasses and serve immediately.

Cucumber Pimm's punch

This tangy blend of freshly juiced cucumber, ginger and apples isn't as innocent as it looks – or tastes. It's lavishly topped with alcohol, so is definitely a drink to enjoy on a lazy summer afternoon. To enjoy on a picnic, just chill the juice really well, pour into a vacuum flask and top up with chilled ginger ale when you reach your destination.

Makes 12 small glasses

1 cucumber
1 lemon
50g/2oz fresh root ginger
4 eating apples
600ml/1 pint/2½ cups Pimm's
sprigs of mint and borage
ice cubes
borage flowers
1.5 litres/2½ pints/6¼ cups ginger ale

1 Cut off a 5cm/2in length from the cucumber and cut into thin slices. Slice the lemon and set both aside.

2 Peel the remaining cucumber and cut it into large chunks. Roughly chop the ginger and apples. Push the apples, then the ginger and cucumber through a juicer and pour the juice into a large jug (pitcher) or bowl.

3 Stir the Pimm's into the juice, add the cucumber, lemon slices and mint and borage sprigs, then chill.

4 Just before serving, add the ice cubes and borage flowers to the punch and top up with ginger ale. Ladle into glasses or glass cups.

Mulled plums in Marsala

You needn't confine mulled drinks to the festive season. This fruity version, distinctively spiced and laced with Marsala, is served chilled, so is perfect for drinks parties at any time of the year. This is a delicious and practical way of using an abundance of sweet, juicy plums to make an exotic drink that is guaranteed to impress your guests.

Makes 4 glasses

500g/1¼lb ripe plums
15g/½oz fresh root ginger, sliced
5ml/1 tsp whole cloves
25g/1oz/2 tbsp light muscovado (brown) sugar
200ml/7fl oz/scant 1 cup Marsala
ice cubes

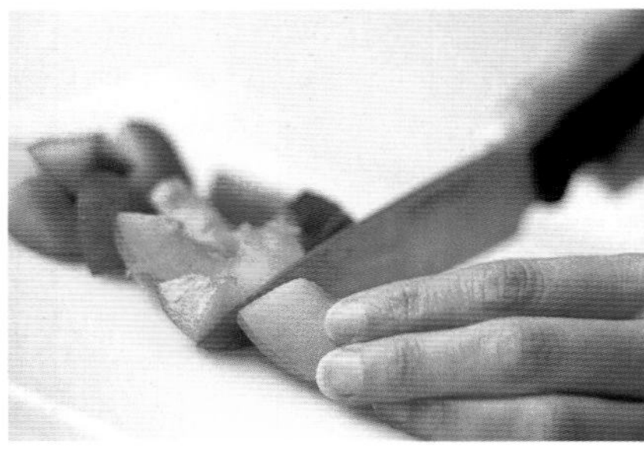

1 Halve two of the plums and discard the stones (pits). Roughly chop the remainder. Put the ginger, cloves and sugar in a small pan with 300ml/½ pint/1¼ cups water. Heat gently until the sugar has dissolved then bring to the boil and add the halved plums.

2 Reduce the heat and simmer gently for 2–3 minutes until the plums have softened but still retain their shape. Using a slotted spoon, lift out the plums and leave the plums and syrup to cool.

3 Push the remaining plums through a juicer. Strain the syrup and mix with the plum juice and Marsala.

4 Put ice cubes and plum halves in four glasses and pour over the syrup. Serve with stirrers, if you like.

Cook's tip

If you are having a party, make a large batch of this drink. It can be transferred to a large punch bowl with a ladle so that your guests can help themselves and fish out the Marsala-soaked plums.

Berried treasure

The combination of cranberries and raspberries is fast becoming a juice classic, despite the fact that these fruits are at their best during different seasons. This needn't hinder you though, just use one in frozen form – the fruit will thaw quickly and save you adding ice. This recipe uses raspberry conserve in place of the more usual sugar or honey to add sweetness.

Makes 2 tall glasses

250g/9oz/1½ cups raspberries
45ml/3 tbsp raspberry conserve
250g/9oz/1½ cups cranberries
soda water (club soda) or sparkling mineral water

1 Push all the raspberries through a juicer, followed by the raspberry conserve and then the cranberries.

2 Pour the juice into tall glasses, top up with soda water or sparkling mineral water and serve immediately.

Cook's tip

For a pretty presentation, thread a few of the berries on to wooden cocktail sticks (toothpicks) and rest them across the rim of the glasses. (To balance the sticks successfully, you'll need to use relatively narrow glasses.)

Index